5 IN 1

KIRSTIN RAE EVANS

PUBLIC SPEAKING

BONUS INSIDE

Engage, Persuade, and Captivate Your Audience by Being an Effective Speaker

91 TECHNIQUES & HACKS
to Boost Your Confidence and Banish Your Anxiety
When Presenting or Debating

© **Copyright 2024 - All rights reserved.**

The content contained within this book may not be reproduced, duplicated or transmitted without direct written permission from the author or the publisher.

Under no circumstances will any blame or legal responsibility be held against the publisher, or author, for any damages, reparation, or monetary loss due to the information contained within this book, either directly or indirectly.

Legal Notice:

This book is copyright protected. It is only for personal use. You cannot amend, distribute, sell, use, quote or paraphrase any part, or the content within this book, without the consent of the author or publisher.

Disclaimer Notice:

Please note the information contained within this document is for educational and entertainment purposes only. All effort has been executed to present accurate, up to date, reliable, complete information. No warranties of any kind are declared or implied. Readers acknowledge that the author is not engaged in the rendering of legal, financial, medical or professional advice. The content within this book has been derived from various sources. Please consult a licensed professional before attempting any techniques outlined in this book.

By reading this document, the reader agrees that under no circumstances is the author responsible for any losses, direct or indirect, that are incurred as a result of the use of the information contained within this document, including, but not limited to, errors, omissions, or inaccuracies.

FREE BONUSES

Thank you for your purchase! Along with your book, you now have exclusive access to five invaluable bonuses designed to enhance your public speaking skills and elevate your confidence.

Here's a glimpse of what you'll receive:

1. **Speak Now:** Daily practices to sharpen your public speaking skills.
2. **Speak Your Path:** A guide to creating your personal development plan for public speaking success.
3. **Speak with Confidence:** A workbook filled with exercises to develop your speaking skills.
4. **Checklist for Confident Public Speaking:** Key steps to prepare for your presentations.
5. **Mindful Speaking:** Techniques connecting mindfulness with public speaking.

To access these bonuses, simply scan the QR code:

Support and Feedback

For feedback, questions, or if you encounter any issues, please visit this link to share your thoughts and get assistance:

https://authorhelpdesk.com/support

TABLE OF CONTENTS

Introduction 9

Book 1: The Power Within 13
    Unleashing Your Confidence
    to Achieve Your Dreams

Book 2: Magnetic Charm 57
    Unleashing Your Inner Charisma
    and Captivating Others

Book 3: The Art of Words 91
    Mastering Speech Preparation
    for Impactful Communication

Book 4: Speak Up and Slay 129
    Overcoming Public Speaking Anxiety
    and Delivering Killer Presentations

Book 5: The Persuasive Speaker 163
    Mastering the Art of Influence
    and Winning Audiences Over

Conclusion 187

Glossary 189

References 191

Introduction

Do you ever feel nervous or anxious during those moments when suddenly confronted with having to speak in front of a group of people? Does just the idea of standing in front of a group of your peers at work or school make your heart race and your palms sweat?

If you have ever felt your mind suddenly go blank when put in the spotlight at work or in school—I am here to tell you that you are not alone. Public speaking anxiety affects millions of people worldwide, and for many, it can represent a significant hurdle in life.

Anxiety, stemming from the fear of public speaking, is a debilitating affliction that can hold you back from achieving your full potential and can even contribute to developing other social and relational complexes that can have devastating effects on your life and your interactions with others.

Not only can struggles with public speaking anxiety prevent you from effectively managing your current life situations—but they can also affect the goals you have set for the future, including your academic pursuits and career trajectory. Worse yet, the anxieties and phobias around public speaking can even creep into your social life and close personal relationships.

I know firsthand how debilitating public speaking anxiety can be. When I first went off to college, I was still a shy, introverted, somewhat naive young girl who had struggled with ADD since grade school.

I began to rely on my medication as a crutch, as the difficulties I had navigating the pressures of college-level studies were compounded by a newly acquired and unwelcome, creeping social anxiety.

While during my college years, I was able to cement bonds with a small, close-knit group of friends, I found it increasingly difficult to relate to my neurotypical classmates, who seemed to tackle their work with ease and were seemingly able to adjust to the new environments and social situations without showing any signs of discomfort.

The realization that I was at a disadvantage to my peers led me down a dark path that impacted my self-esteem. To combat my growing sense of inferiority, I would stay up all night to cram for exams and work on projects, hoping that by putting my nose to the grindstone, I would come out on top.

I have always considered myself a diligent "type A" person, but it was during my late teens and early 20s, that my obsession with performance and optimization went to extreme levels.

I tried everything, from transcendental meditation to following an ayurvedic diet, but it was not until I started to focus on developing my innate skills and working on my self-confidence that I began to see real progress.

This is one of the most important messages that I want to convey to you: *that there is no quick fix or magical pill to overcome social anxiety and public speaking struggles.* It requires hard work, determination, and a willingness to face your fears head-on.

I believe that by sharing my story and my personal struggle, I can now help others who may be experiencing similar difficulties, inspiring them to take the necessary steps to improve their public speaking skills and overcome their anxiety.

Over the years, I have learned that with the right mindset and tools, anyone can overcome their public speaking anxiety and deliver powerful messages, speeches, and presentations with confidence and charisma. The product of those countless years of struggle I went through is this book.

In the pages that follow, I will provide you with some practical solutions and tips to help you unleash your inner charisma, boost your self-confidence, and help you become a persuasive speaker who can captivate and influence your audience.

Through the five different books contained in this volume, you will learn the essentials of public speaking that I believe are crucial to becoming a successful speaker. You will find 91 techniques, tips, and strategies to mold yourself into the persuasive, confident speaker you have always dreamed of becoming. It's peppered throughout the entire book and it's intentionally designed this way to serve as your guide along each step of the process.

First, we will start by exploring the power of confidence and how to unleash it to achieve your dreams. Then, we will delve into the art of charisma and how to captivate your audience with your newly-acquired magnetic presence. Next, we will move on to tackling the challenge of speech preparation and how to master your message for maximum impact.

Throughout the entirety of this book, we will also be taking a direct, holistic approach to address the crippling side effects of public speaking anxiety and providing practical tips and techniques for overcoming them and delivering killer presentations.

Whether you are naturally introverted or extroverted, you are sure to find techniques within this book that can help you become the best version of yourself and deliver killer speeches that will capture your audience with the powerful, meaningful words you share with them.

In the final book, we will discuss the art of influence and persuasion and how to use your public speaking skills to win over your audience and achieve your goals. By the end of this book, you will have a comprehensive understanding of the key elements of public speaking and how to leverage them to become a confident and persuasive speaker.

So, by now, you are probably eager to start taking a look at how to take your public speaking skills to the next level; let's get started!

Book 1: The Power Within

Unleashing Your Confidence
to Achieve Your Dreams

Kirsten Rae Evans

TABLE OF CONTENTS

Introduction 17

Chapter 1: On Self-Esteem and Self-Confidence 19
    Reasons For Low Self Esteem 21
    Reasons For Lack of Self-Confidence 25

Chapter 2: Self-Confident Individuals 35
    Traits of an Insecure Individual 35
    Traits of a Confident Individual 42
    Benefits of Confidence 45

Chapter 3: Boosting Confidence 49
    Steps to Regain Confidence 49
    Adjusting Your Thought Process 50
    Ways to Build Confidence 50

Introduction

The ability to believe in oneself is a powerful tool for achieving success. Confidence is the foundation on which we build our dreams and pursue our goals. When we lack it, we become hesitant, doubtful, and afraid to take risks.

However, when we unleash our inner force, we become unstoppable, and the world opens up to us in ways we never thought possible.

In this book, we will explore the power of confidence and how to cultivate it within ourselves. We will discuss the mindset and habits necessary to build and maintain it, even in the face of adversity.

Through practical tips, exercises, and real-life examples, I will show you how to unleash your innate inner drive, tapping into your unharnessed potential to achieve your dreams. So, let's dive in and discover how to unlock the power within!

Chapter 1
On Self-Esteem and Self-Confidence

Self-confidence is a vital component of our well-being and is closely intertwined and related to our internal levels of self-esteem. These two internal senses are necessities—crucial parts of our internal realities that must be developed to healthy levels during our childhoods to function properly later as healthy, well-adjusted adults.

While these essential senses begin developing within all of us early in life, it does not mean that once we are older, we can start to neglect the importance of developing and maintaining them. In fact, cultivating and maintaining our levels of Self-esteem and Self-confidence requires a proactive effort on our part.

Possessing the Power to Know Ourselves

Possessing the power to know ourselves is the first step towards fully integrating this idea and putting it into practice in our own lives. The first step is to realize that during the moments when our self-esteem is lowest, our confidence tends to suffer as well.

The Power of Positive Thinking

If you have ever had moments in life where your thinking becomes clouded and gloomy and you constantly dwell on negativity—well, you know what I am talking about.

While a negative outlook on life can be caused by depression, trauma, or other psychological realities (things that we we will also be discussing within this chapter), sometimes what we are really struggling with the most is ourselves.

Self-Care

Sometimes we are our own worst enemy when it comes to being aware of, regulating, and caring for our self-esteem and self-confidence. While we all have different baseline levels of these senses, their levels can fluctuate as we go through life and are confronted with new challenges, disappointments, and failures.

Our ability to cope with these difficult moments, to roll with the punches, and most importantly, to be in touch with our inner selves is where the opportunities lie for improvement and personal growth.

What we'll learn

In this chapter, we will be exploring the most common reasons why people struggle with issues of low self-esteem and lack of self-confidence. While the themes covered in this book are meant to help you take account of why your self-esteem may be in shabby shape—it is essential to keep in mind that they are not intended to criticize or critique your character, past behaviors or mistakes in any way.

The issues discussed in this chapter are problems we all struggle with, and we all must confront at some time or another. Honest discussions such as these can be triggering to some but confronting them head-on is the most effective way to make sure that we address the consequences of the ingrained thought patterns and reluctance to change them that we all get tied up in from time to time. So, please take a deep breath and get ready as we delve into a journey into the inner workings of our precious and unique psyches!

Reasons For Low Self Esteem

Low self-esteem can be caused by several factors, including:

- Anxiety and depression
- Genetic makeup
- Life experiences
- Misinformation and misconceptions
- Social media
- Perfectionism

Anxiety and Depression

Generalized anxiety and depression can severely impact a person's self-confidence by causing negative thought patterns that can ultimately manifest themselves as a lack of self-worth. If you have ever found yourself dealing with these common psychological afflictions—you are not alone. In fact, according to the National Institute of Mental Health (2017), over 30% of Americans suffer from an anxiety disorder at least one point during their lives.

While severe depression is significantly less prevalent than anxiety disorders, affecting less than 10% of U.S. adults (Beck, et al., 2011), it still represents a serious problem in most developed western countries.

Depression contributes to costly drains on public health systems and worker productivity (Simon et al., 2000), and most importantly, it exerts a profound effect on the general health, mental well-being, quality of life, and length of life of the people afflicted with it.

Genetic Makeup

Genetics come into play when it comes to a predisposition towards developing anxiety and depression and also towards the ability to develop healthy levels of self-esteem. It is thought that generational trauma and the depressive and anxious traits that can come with them can be passed on from generation to generation.

Genetics can determine to some extent, the amount of confidence-boosting chemicals our brain can access, making it possible that some people simply have to put more effort into building and maintaining healthy levels of self-esteem. It is also thought that much of our capacity for cultivating and upholding self-esteem originates in early childhood development, making our faculties highly dependent on our upbringing.

After all, our parents or caretakers contribute most heavily to the attachment styles we develop in early childhood, and which carry on through adulthood. The coping skills we develop and our capacity for maintaining healthy levels as adults have much to do with the messages, we receive from the caretaker figures in our lives from an early age.

Life Experiences

The unique and individual life experiences we all go through, such as trauma, bullying, harassment, and discrimination, can also contribute to our baseline self-esteem levels.

Victims of abuse, whether physical or emotional, can be presented with unique challenges in attempts to build and maintain healthy levels of self-esteem later in life and must often develop skills to aid in cultivating self-worth that looks past their traumas.

If you have been a victim of abuse or have dealt with serious trauma, it is essential to get the right help. Often through therapy or other types of counseling, you can develop ways to process your trauma healthily while helping you move on from the difficult experiences you have been through.

Social Media

The prevalence of social media and social media campaigns, with their curated, highly edited versions of people's lives in particular, can contribute to feelings of inadequacy and insecurity. Especially for young women, the pressures of social media can lead to body-image issues, which in turn affect our innate levels of self-esteem.

Additionally, social media platforms provide the ability for misinformation and misconceptions to be spread with ease. As false, sometimes damaging ideas are seeded and allowed to flourish, users are vulnerable to their influence and the effects they can exert on their self-esteem both directly and indirectly.

Misinformation and Misconceptions

Misinformation and misconceptions, particularly about what it truly means to be confident, can create unrealistic expectations and self-doubt in individuals struggling with self-esteem issues.

Understanding the true meaning of self-confidence and self-esteem is crucial, regardless of whether societal, cultural, or systemic factors have influenced our perceptions and beliefs about them.

Having and displaying true confidence is not about being the proudest, the most show-off, or being the best at something—rather, it is about being comfortable with yourself, not being afraid to be vulnerable, and being willing to show your whole being and essence, flaws included.

Perfectionism

While it may seem contradictory: Striving for perfectionism, or rather, working towards being your "optimized most-capable self," often at the expense of neglecting other equally important facets of your life, can be a good way to set yourself up for disappointment. It can also damage your self-esteem.

That is right! Focusing too much on yourself and trying to become self-actualized rather than self-accepting can lead you down the wrong path. Not only can it affect your relationships with others, but if you focus 100% of your time on trying to "improve" yourself, your flaws or perceived flaws will always be at the forefront of your mind. Who wants that?

Moreover, the idea of "perfectionism" itself is a form of faulty thinking, which can lead to obsessiveness, procrastination, and constant self-doubt. So give yourself a break; self-love, after all, is more important and much more satisfying than misguided attempts at perfection.

Self-Esteem vs. Self-Confidence

While developing and maintaining healthy levels of self-esteem is an enormous undertaking in itself, it is only one part of the picture. The next step is to take a look at your self-confidence and assess where you are with this important aspect of beautiful you!

Reasons For Lack of Self-Confidence

Self-confidence is different from self-esteem. Though related, it is a facet of ourselves that is a bit easier to access. Surprisingly—we can almost turn it on and off at will. It is best defined as our ability to believe in ourselves. Once you wrap your head around that concept, you will find its power to be life-changing!

Wielding our self-confidence by actively upholding and maintaining it allows us to access it as a tool when we need those extra boosts that will make or break us getting through challenging moments in life. When we fail in life, as we all do from time to time, we risk compromising our self-confidence.

But failure itself is not the problem. It is our inability to address our own failure that so often gets us in trouble.

What Happens When We Fail?

In failing to take the steps to properly address and process and to accept the truths about what went wrong when we *do* fail or make a mistake, we are doing a great disservice to ourselves that runs the risk of putting our own self-confidence in check.

When we fail, we too often tend to blame ourselves or others rather than confront the sometimes embarrassing or honest reasons behind our failure. It is often this very denial that can erode our internal belief system that is meant to uphold our self-confidence levels.

Learning how to have and maintain self-confidence is all about letting yourself fail and being okay with it—but most importantly, being accountable to yourself and others.

There are a whole range of other factors that can drive a lack of self-confidence, and while some of them may be triggering, they are important concepts to think about and to begin incorporating into your self-perception and self-analysis.

If you have ever struggled with any of the following issues: know that you are not alone and that they are common issues that we all can struggle with from time to time.

The issues that we will be touching on in this chapter are:

- Social anxiety and avoidance of social interactions
- Comparing oneself with others
- Lack of personal integrity
- Lack of purpose in life
- Lack of self-acceptance
- Lack of self-belief
- People-pleasing
- Giving up too soon
- Using the wrong approach

Social Anxiety and Avoidance of Social Interactions

Avoiding social interactions can prevent us from developing some of the crucial social skills that assist us in navigating life and allow us to maintain good relationships with our peers and others. This neglect, over time, can develop into a problem and can lead to manifestations of a further lack of self-confidence in social situations.

While it is common for many of us to struggle with anxiety of one type or another at some point in our lives, for some, anxiety around social interaction and situations can become so severe that it can turn into a more serious affliction. Severe cases and instances of social anxiety are recognized as full-fledged anxiety disorders by the DSM-5.

Building and maintaining healthy levels of social interactions and possessing the ability to navigate many different types of social situations with ease make it easier for us to uphold our self-confidence.

If you have struggled with social anxiety or feel unable to relate socially to your peers and others, know that help is available, and there are many tools out there to help build up or repair your social skills, including counseling and occupational therapy.

Comparing Yourself to Others

Comparing yourself to others can also lead to feelings of inadequacy and self-doubt. In today's day and age, these tendencies can be exacerbated by social media, as discussed in the previous section under the "social media" heading.

While it is always possible to find someone who seems to have it all and can seemingly navigate life with ease—if you have ever had the chance to speak to one of these "perfect seeming" individuals on a heart-to-heart level, you would know that they, like you are not without their own problems and challenges.

The realization that we are all in this thing called life together, all with our unique struggles to get through, is what we must grasp to stop comparing our lives to our perceived versions of the lives of others.

Only once we stop comparing ourselves to others can we truly exude strong self-confidence. This does not mean that we should not admire others; there is nothing wrong with aspiring to follow certain aspects of what you see others doing. The main thing here is to recognize your individuality and uniqueness is your best asset.

Lack of Personal Integrity

A lack of personal integrity can create inner conflict and contribute to a lack of self-confidence. If you have ever lied in a way that hurt others or have engaged in other types of deceitful deeds such as cheating, misrepresentation, or inauthenticity, you may be stoking your internal conflict.

Aside from the effects these types of personal integrity breaches have on others, they can wear on your well-being. If you are naturally inclined towards conniving impulses, and relish in lying and cheating in ways that grate on others, then you may have a few things to work on in the personal integrity department.

Lack of Purpose in Life

A lack of purpose in life can be faced at multiple points throughout our own unique journeys in life. Have you ever experienced a job loss or felt directionless or stuck in life and in your day-to-day existence?

While it is common to lose sight of our goals and to feel as if we do not know what we are doing in life, it is important to have a well-defined sense of purpose, whether you find that as a parent, as a worker, as a creative, or by pursuing your passions towards hobbies and learning new skills—there is no predefined way to do it.

Everyone is on their own quest in life, but sometimes we get off-track. When this inevitably happens at one point or another in our lives, it can lead to feelings of emptiness and a deficiency of our inner self-confidence.

Lack of Self-Acceptance

Self-acceptance is one of the keys to life. While related to the previous discussions of perfectionism and dealing with failure in a healthy way—the idea of self-acceptance goes beyond just being easy on yourself.

We are all flawed and beautiful in different ways. Why, you ask? Because we are human! Though it may sound obvious, the true reason why we all must work towards radical self-acceptance is a simple fact: We are the way we are.

Now, you might think that the concept of radical self-acceptance runs the risk of going contrary to the ever-important idea of self-improvement. This, however, is not the case. A big part of self-acceptance is the realization that things are constantly in flux.

You are never going to be stuck in the same situations and the same modes of thinking that are bogging you down again. Why? Because we as humans are resilient and adaptable, and most importantly: we possess the capacity to change, to improve, and to reinvent ourselves, sometimes even multiple times throughout our lifetimes!

It is about accepting yourself for who you are now, in this very moment, throughout your darkest moments: forever.

Lack of Belief in Yourself

As discussed before, self-confidence itself is a belief. When your belief in yourself and your capacities to succeed, to overcome, and to be resilient in the face of significant obstacles is compromised—so too is the very core of your inner being.

Believing in yourself does not mean you must ever ignore the sheer magnitude of the problems you face in life, and it does not mean that we should be blindly optimistic and hopeful. What it means is that we all must cultivate and find things like hope and optimism, and positivity in the most unexpected places, and we must do so in our own unique, individual ways.

Cultivating and maintaining a deep belief in yourself only requires a few things: that you have an underlying will to grow stronger, to persevere, and to develop as a unique, nuanced individual. If you lack either of the essential drives, which we can all struggle with from time to time, it may be time to seek counseling or therapy.

There is no shame in admitting that you are deficient in any of these drives. Life can get us all down, and at many times throughout our lives, it can be difficult to get back on our feet or even to feel like ourselves again.

People-Pleasing

People-pleasing is a pitfall that many of us have fallen victim to at various points throughout our lives. While it sounds like it would be a positive trait to exhibit, in fact—satisfying the wants and desires of others can sometimes be a negative thing. That is right!

The problem is we sometimes attempt to please others at our own expense, and this is where the difficulty can arise.

When we over-extend or over-exert ourselves, bending over backward to satisfy the needs of others, we need to do so in a healthy way—one in which we have clear boundaries established. If not, we run the risk of exhausting ourselves, depleting ourselves of the very energy we possess, the caring, compassionate energy that we very much *do* wish to extend to others.

If we are concerned with pleasing others at our own expense, then we have a problem that can affect our levels of self-confidence. While helping and being involved in the lives of others can be satisfying and can contribute to our sense of wholeness and usefulness, it can also detract time away from the vital self-care and self-maintenance routines.

Giving Up Too Soon

Why is it that we often turn away from things right before we strike gold?

It is not an issue of luck but rather one of determination, of commitment, and of fortitude. Across all facets of life, this is a common occurrence—somehow, we have an innate tendency to give up right before breakthroughs are able to happen.

Though the psychology behind this phenomenon is difficult to pin down, much of it can be attributed to our benefits and reward system.

For all our hard work in life, we naturally expect that we will be able to reap some kind of reward from it. That, however, is not always the case, and in many instances, we have to struggle for years before our ideas or goals finally come to fruition.

The paradox here lies in the balance between patience and throwing in the towel. It is often the most stubborn people who refuse to give up and eventually break through. This stubbornness, however, must be one with intent behind it because blind stubbornness can lead to failure just as easily as it can lead to a meaningful, life-changing breakthrough.

If you have ever given up on something too soon and later regretted it: you can see where this is going. In life, we must give things our all before abandoning them, and even then, sometimes, in retrospect, it seems like we made the wrong choice.

Giving up too soon on things can lead down the rocky road towards self-doubt, which can lead us to doubt our own self-confidence.

Using the Wrong Approach

Using the wrong approach to deal with situations can also contribute to a lack of self-confidence. If you have ever felt like you have acted in error or have ever made a mistake in general, welcome to the club.

These minor transgressions are the things we do every day, and I am here to tell you: there is nothing inherently wrong with being wrong.

What is wrong, however, is being wrong about something and not being aware of it or being in denial over it. Making and learning from our mistakes is an essential part of succeeding in life.

When we make the same mistakes over and over again, we are ignoring the truths that are being revealed to us. While it is easy to fall back on old habits and rely on ingrained modes of thinking and doing, overreliance on what *we know* or *what we think we know* can take us down a dark path.

You may have heard before that there is *"no wrong way"* to do so-and-so things. Well, I am sorry to break the news to you, but that is simply not true. There are many people out there that constantly deal with tasks, situations, and interpersonal relationships in ways that are self-damaging and contribute to eroding our character.

There *is* a wrong way to do things, and many of us find that out the wrong way, continually making the same mistakes repeatedly.

These repeated instances of failure can lead to a disintegration of our self-confidence. The more and more we make mistakes that we do not learn from, the more life feels like swinging blindly at a piñata.

If you have ever felt this way, I would like to pose the following question: What if the piñata were not even there in the first place? Batting blindly is no way to go forward in life. We cannot simply continue to swing blindly at life, with the only feedback received from our misguided attempts being that we have not yet contacted the surface.

We all need feedback and validation to move forward in life. These are essential tools that we receive from others and from our own senses as we move forward, as we change, and as we learn from our experiences.

When we keep making the same mistakes over and over again, we are doing a disservice not just to ourselves but to those around us. Moreover, the toll that our constant unaddressed, unresolved mistake-making takes on us and those close to us can make it difficult for us to cultivate and maintain the levels of self-confidence and self-esteem we need to thrive and coexist with others in healthy, constructive ways.

To Sum Things Up

As we have examined in this chapter, there are a multitude of reasons why individuals may struggle with self-confidence and self-esteem. Identifying and understanding these factors is an essential step in developing strategies to improve our confidence and overall well-being so that once we have worked on the issues holding us back, we can reap the benefits of having high levels of self-confidence.

Chapter 2
Self-Confident Individuals

The benefits of taking a proactive role in building and maintaining our levels of self-confidence are numerous! By comparing the traits exhibited by insecure vs. secure individuals, we can gain great insight into the psychology behind maintaining healthy levels of self-esteem and self-confidence.

Have you ever wondered why some people seem to radiate confidence effortlessly while others struggle to maintain their composure even in the most mundane situations? The difference between these two individuals lies in their level of self-confidence. In this chapter, we will explore the benefits of self-confidence and understand the traits that differentiate an insecure individual from a confident one.

Traits of an Insecure Individual

We will discuss the importance of self-confidence and how it can improve your life in many ways. One of the common contributors to low self-confidence is insecurity.

Insecurity can manifest itself in many ways, and it can be difficult for us all to admit to ourselves the moments that we have been insecure. However difficult it may be to confront our own weaknesses, it is important to identify and address these issues before they wreak havoc on your life.

The common traits of insecure individuals that we will be touching upon in this section include:

- They act like a know-it-all.
- They are afraid of change.
- They blame others for their own mistakes.
- They are close-minded.
- They hide their flaws.
- They are indecisive.
- They are jealous of others' success.
- They are judgmental.
- They make excuses.
- They are pessimistic.

Acting Like a Know-It-All

Insecure individuals often pretend to have all the answers, even if they do not, to avoid looking stupid or presenting themselves as vulnerable in front of others. If you have ever pretended to understand a reference someone made that you are not actually familiar with, or you have lied or mischaracterized your level of understanding of a concept or issue, you have been guilty of this transgression.

It is nothing to be ashamed of, however, and in the kind of high-drive high-performance culture we live in, it is a common place to find ourselves, whether in academic contexts or in the workplace.

We are constantly surrounded by others, some of whom will be more intelligent, more adept, and better able to articulate themselves than we are. It is a completely natural impulse driven by our competitive nature to pretend that we understand things that seem to come naturally to others. We strive to be recognized as being on the same level as our peers, and we yearn to feel connected to them.

While there is nothing wrong with showing enthusiasm about a subject that we are novices at or with diving into an amateurish pursuit without questioning our own knowledge basis, there are moments when we all have been guilty of fudging the numbers a bit. It is an essential part of human nature, our coping, adapting, and socialization skills, to sometimes pretend that we know what we do not.

In resisting the urge to be a know-it-all, however, we *can* make ourselves vulnerable and more open to absorbing the accumulated knowledge of those around us.

When we are brave enough to admit to others what we do not know, we are not only practicing radical honesty, but we are also making strides towards becoming secure and self-actualized, whole individuals.

Being Afraid of Change

Change is inevitable, but insecure individuals are afraid of the unknown and avoid taking risks, which can prevent them from growing personally and professionally. The fear of change stems from the fact that change can easily be perceived as a threat to our security.

Getting comfortable with routine and predictability is one of the essential things that allows us to maintain balance in our lives. Still, our innate tendency to seek comfort can also, at times, become a chain that prevents us from ascending to higher places.

The fears of the unknown and the unfamiliar are innate impulses that we all hold to varying degrees. From birth, we are conditioned to gain comfort from the familiar: from the face and embrace of our mother or caretaker figure. From a young age, the sight of unfamiliar faces and the terror that unfamiliar environments can bring great distress.

From an evolutionary standpoint, our innate fears have served us well in certain areas, while they have hindered our growth in others. The innate fear of the unknown and the unfamiliar that we possess on a primal, evolutionary level is what kept us safe from predators, from hostile threats from outsiders, and what kept us living in close-knit groups and support networks that we rely on for both emotional need and physical safety.

What we must all do as individuals is to be mindful of the delicate balance between our comfort-seeking impulses and our capacities for going out on a limb and risk-taking that characterize our very humanness. Being aware of and striking the right balance between these genetic and socially-ingrained modes of behavior allows us to transcend our innate sense of fear and embrace change and progress in healthy, productive ways.

Blaming Others for Their Own Mistakes

Instead of taking responsibility for their actions, insecure individuals tend to blame others for their mistakes to avoid negative consequences. From childhood, we are conditioned to shift our culpability onto others; if you grew up with siblings as I did—you know what I am talking about.

Once we reach adulthood, the blame game can only get us so far. There comes a point in all of our lives where we must start owning up to our mistakes to continue moving forward.

Being Close-Minded

Insecure individuals have a fixed mindset and are not open to new ideas, which can severely limit their growth and progress. Aside from the fact that living a small, closed existence can make us feel constricted and unable to move forward in life, more often than not, in today's world, close-mindedness is seen as a highly negative character trait.

From academia to the corporate workplace—rhetoric around the idea of open-mindedness is widespread and often plays a key role in the goals and objectives set by institutions and businesses. The types of people that do well in these dynamic environments, from research institutions to corporate boardrooms, are people who have an open mind and an open approach.

So, if you want to participate in the world at large and are having difficulties breaking through in the work world or your academic trajectory, you may want to check your levels of close-minded behavior. Being close-minded in today's culture is a sure way to increase the odds that you will be pushed toward the margins and excluded from participating in many exciting, dynamic fields and pursuits.

Hiding Their Flaws

Insecure individuals are afraid of being judged, so they try to hide their flaws and imperfections from others. Sometimes this manifests itself as overachievement or acting like a know-it-all, and other times it takes the form of passivity or reluctance to participate. The driving reason why insecure people hide their flaws is the same, no matter how it is presented. A deep-seated inferiority complex is a driving factor behind this type of behavior.

Being obsessive over our personal appearance, how we come off to others, or being ashamed of our levels of competency at certain things can cause us to depend on cover-up exercises to conceal these perceived flaws and deficits from those around us. In doing so, we are not being honest with ourselves and end up shooting ourselves in the foot.

Hiding our flaws makes us emotionally closed off to others, and clamping down on our outward displays of vulnerability can make us come off as cold or unfriendly. Furthermore, if we become overly concerned with keeping our flaws under wraps, we become less likely to seek the help and guidance of others, which is an essential part of developing and maintaining healthy relationships with others.

Being Indecisive

Insecure individuals find it challenging to make decisions, as they are afraid of making the wrong choice and being judged for it. They are often not even aware of their own likes and dislikes, as outside opinions are a major factor in driving and determining their decision-making processes. This type of herd-following mentality can have detrimental effects.

Indecision signals to others that we lack security and do not have confidence in our decision-making abilities. It can also signal that we are not sure of our internal value systems or lack substance behind the driving motivations that we outwardly present to others.

Being Jealous of Others' Success

Insecure individuals are often envious of the success of others, finding it difficult to celebrate the achievements of their peers and even sometimes those of their own family members. Considering other people's achievements as an affront to their own failures or inability to succeed—these types of people are an unfortunate lot who can be a real drag on things in any context, whether it be at work, school, or home.

Jealous people consider others their rivals and thrive off an unhealthy sense of competition. This competitive spirit, in reality, is just an exercise in trying to stay ahead and afloat, always maintaining the upper edge over their "weaker" competitors, who, in many cases, are, in fact, stronger and more well-equipped.

Attempting to fill the deep gaps in their own personal psyche, these sad figures who wallow in jealousy run the risk of driving themselves down the path to failure.

Being Judgmental

Insecure individuals tend to judge others to boost their own feelings of superiority. In reality, these impulses are driven by the deep-seated insecurities they hold about themselves. In their judgment of others, they seek to rectify their own perceived flaws and failings through the act of critiquing or criticizing others' behaviors, beliefs, and values.

Being judgmental is something that would not win you many friends. Aside from its socially isolating tendencies, it simply is not a sound practice to uphold. Those who constantly police their peer group or attack the character of those around them run the risk of isolating and alienating themselves from others.

Making Excuses

Insecure individuals tend to make excuses for their inappropriate or insensitive behavior, their inaction, and, often, for their mistakes. This allows them to evade negative feedback and criticism that can be damaging to their fragile personalities. Excuse-filled behavior is easy to conceal in the form of analytical responses to questions or dilemmas that break down problems on a technical level.

Insecure individuals who are highly adept at excuse-making will often use their technical and analytical proficiencies to shirk responsibility. By explaining away, they can convince others and themselves that they are not responsible for their own actions or failings.

Pessimism

Nobody likes to be around a "Negative Nancy." If you have ever had to be around or work on a project with someone like this, you know what I am talking about. Insecure individuals have a negative outlook on life and are constantly anticipating the worst-case scenario—something which can make them impossible to be around and collaborate with effectively.

Insecure individuals are inherently pessimistic because it lets them off the hook when things do go wrong, as they always inevitably do. By setting up the preconditions for blame-shifting, they know that by calling attention to the fact that an undertaking will fail, they will be able to deflect culpability before the necessity to do so even arises.

My Own Struggle

I have certainly had my own moments where I felt insecure and exhibited some of these traits. I often felt like I needed to know everything, even when I did not. I also struggled with decision-making and tended to be pessimistic about the outcome of situations.

Through conscious effort, however, I was able to overcome my own insecurities and break free of the chains that were holding me back from success and the realization of my own full potential.

Traits of a Confident Individual

Confidence can be learned and developed over time. A confident individual radiates self-assurance, and with just a few tweaks to the way you approach things, you can too!

The common traits exhibited by confident individuals are as follows:

- They possess the ability to make complex decisions.
- They always accept responsibility for their actions.

- They always admit to their own mistakes.
- They are always learning and growing.
- They celebrate the success of others.
- They possess the ability to laugh at themselves.
- They are open-minded.
- They exude optimism and have an optimistic outlook on life.
- They take risks.

The Ability to Make Complex Decisions

Confident individuals are able to effectively envision and execute complex decision-making-based tasks. They trust their own abilities and innate sense of judgment across a broad range of issues.

Accepting Responsibility for Actions and Admitting to Mistakes

Confident individuals take responsibility for their actions. In turn, this proactive owning-up behavior helps reinforce their accountability and credibility among their peers, improving the prospects for positive future outcomes. Likewise, confident individuals are not afraid to admit their mistakes. In fact, being honest about their mistakes is often what helps them gain and reinforce the respect they have from others.

Always Learning and Growing

Confident individuals have a growth-oriented mindset and are always eager to learn new things. This desire and willingness to learn and change helps bolster their skills and knowledge while allowing them to dynamically shift and adapt to new, unfamiliar situations.

Celebrating the Success of Others

Confident individuals celebrate others' success, as they understand that success is not a zero-sum game and that there are more than enough accolades to go around. They patiently await their turn, knowing that one day it will be their time to shine and bask in their own success.

The Ability to Laugh at Oneself

Confident individuals have the ability to laugh at themselves and their own mistakes. This allows them to bring levity to moments where self-doubt and self-criticism can easily creep in, allowing them to maintain a positive outlook on life without getting bogged down on their failings.

Being Open-Minded

Confident individuals are open to new ideas and perspectives, which helps them cement new relationships with other open-minded, dynamic people and leads to progress. Opening up new doors and new opportunities, confident individuals remain open-minded not just for strategic gain but to be well-positioned to let inspiration in.

Being Optimistic

Confident individuals have an optimistic outlook on life and believe that things will ultimately work out in their favor. The power of positive thinking is what gets them through the moments of turbulence and tribulation in life.

Taking Risks

Confident individuals are not afraid to take risks. Risk-taking minimizes the possibility of missed opportunities and helps them achieve their overarching objectives and dreams.

The Power of Confidence

As someone who has worked hard to develop my confidence, I can attest to the power of these traits. Learning to take responsibility for my actions and being willing to admit my mistakes has been a game-changer for me. Celebrating the successes of others and being open to learning from them has also helped me grow and improve as a person. The ability to stay optimistic through my darkest moments is what allowed me to come out on top, and my ability to take leaps of faith is what got me to where I am today.

Benefits of Confidence

Radiating confidence has numerous benefits that can positively impact your personal and professional life. Confidence is a state of mind that can have a significant impact on your behavior, emotions, and thoughts. Here are some ways in which confidence can benefit you:

The benefits of having high levels of confidence that we will be touching upon in this section include:

- Your ideas will be able to influence others.
- You will become more action-oriented.
- You will be happier in life and will exhibit more gratitude.
- You will become more resilient.
- You will feel valued and respected.
- You will have greater freedom from social anxiety.
- You will be able to maintain healthier relationships.
- You will be able to perform your best, even under stress.
- Your openness to new experiences will increase.
- You will be able to exhibit high levels of leadership skills and executive presence.
- You will radiate positive behavior, inspiring those around you.
- Your negative thoughts and modes of thinking will drift away.

Having Your Ideas Make an Impact on Others

Confident individuals can influence others with their ideas and actions, which can help them achieve their goals. People tend to gravitate towards people who exhibit high levels of confidence and are more likely to trust them and follow their lead.

Becoming More Action-Oriented

Confident individuals act and do not wait for opportunities to come to them. They are more likely to take risks and pursue their goals with determination and enthusiasm, making them more attractive, charismatic individuals.

Being Happier in Life and Exhibiting More Gratitude

Confidence allows individuals to have a positive outlook on life, which helps them maintain a happy and healthy existence. People who are self-confident tend to express higher levels of gratitude for what they have, which further reinforces their overall life satisfaction.

Becoming More Resilient

Confident individuals are better equipped to handle setbacks and challenges as they believe in themselves and their abilities. They are less likely to give up in the face of adversity and are more likely to bounce back from setbacks.

Feeling Valued and Respected

Confidence can help you feel more valued and respected by others. When you radiate confidence, people are more likely to view you as competent, capable, and worthy of respect.

Greater Freedom From Social Anxiety

Confidence can help you overcome social anxiety and shyness. People with high levels of self-confidence are more comfortable in social situations, which allows them to engage more freely with others.

Maintaining Healthier Relationships

Confidence can help you maintain healthier relationships with others. Confident people are more likely to express their needs and opinions, which allows for open and honest communication.

Performing Your Best, Even When Under Stress

Confidence allows individuals to perform at their best, even under stressful circumstances. People with higher levels of self-confidence are better equipped to manage stress and are less likely to be overwhelmed by pressure.

Confidence can improve our performance in various areas of our life, including academics, sports, and work. People who are successfully able to build and maintain higher levels of self-confidence tend to be more focused and motivated, which allows them to achieve their goals more effectively.

Being Open to New Experiences

Confidence can help you become more open to new experiences and opportunities. Self-confident people are more likely to try new things and explore new avenues, which can lead to personal growth and development.

Improving Leadership Skills and Executive Presence.

Confidence is a key characteristic of effective leaders. Self-confident individuals are better equipped to inspire and motivate others, which allows them to exhibit high levels of leadership skills and executive presence.

The Effect of Positive Behavior on Those Around You

Confidence can have a positive impact on those around you. When a person radiates confidence, they are capable of inspiring others to be more confident and to believe in themselves.

Combating Negative Modes of Thinking

Confidence can help you overcome negative thoughts and modes of thinking. People with higher levels of self-confidence tend to have a more positive outlook on life, which allows them to focus on their strengths and accomplishments rather than their weaknesses and failures.

I know how daunting it can be to try new things or put yourself in unfamiliar situations. However, developing confidence can help you overcome those fears and enjoy life more fully. It can also help you improve your relationships with others and achieve your goals.

Confidence is a valuable asset in life, and it can be developed and improved with practice. By learning to exhibit the traits of a confident individual, you can enjoy the many benefits that come with being self-assured and secure in yourself and your abilities!

CHAPTER 3
BOOSTING CONFIDENCE

Are you struggling to regain your confidence? Do not worry, you are not alone. Many people face challenges when it comes to their confidence levels. We will discuss some ways to help you regain your lost confidence.

The confidence-boosting strategies and techniques that we will be touching upon in this chapter include

- Being able to recognize situations that affect your self-esteem.
- Becoming more aware of your thoughts and beliefs.
- Challenging your negative thinking.
- Adjusting your thought process.

Steps to Regain Confidence

To regain confidence, do the following:

Recognizing Situations that Affect Your Self-Esteem

It is essential to identify what situations trigger your insecurity. For instance, social events or public speaking engagements may be sources of anxiety. By understanding what affects your self-esteem, you can prepare yourself to handle these situations better.

Being More Aware of Your Thoughts and Beliefs

The next step is to understand the negative beliefs and thoughts that are contributing to your lack of confidence. This self-reflection will help you understand your thinking patterns and their effects on your confidence.

Challenging Negative Thinking

There are different types of negative thinking that can impact your self-esteem, including all-or-nothing thinking, converting positives into negatives, jumping to negative conclusions, mental filtering, mistaking feelings for facts, and negative self-talk. It is important to challenge these thoughts and replace them with positive ones.

Adjusting Your Thought Process

It is also essential to adjust your thoughts to improve your self-esteem. You can do this by avoiding 'should' and 'must' statements, considering what you have learned, encouraging yourself, focusing on the positive, forgiving yourself, relabeling upsetting thoughts, and using hopeful statements.

Ways to Build Confidence

Aside from the steps we can take to boost our own confidence, there are several things we can do to build and fortify it. In this section, we will discuss some ways to help you strengthen the innate confidence that we all possess.

The confidence-building strategies and techniques that we will be touching upon in this section include:

- Doing more of the things that bring you happiness and satisfaction in life.

- Doing the right thing and practicing radical openness and transparency.
- Not caring so much about what others think.
- Adjusting your thought process.
- Being able to confront your fears.
- Practicing follow-through in all endeavors.
- Getting sh*t done.
- Giving yourself a glow-up.
- Knowing when to say "no," and setting boundaries.
- Living in a way that reflects your values and principles.
- Monitoring your progress.
- Practicing gratitude daily.
- Harnessing the powers of positive self-talk.
- Setting realistic goals for yourself.
- Smiling more often.
- Standing up for yourself and standing tall in the face of obstacles.
- Stopping making comparisons to others.
- Surrounding yourself with positive people and influences.
- Taking care of your physical and mental well-being.
- Thinking long-term and planning for what the bright future may bring.

Do More of What Makes You Happy

Doing what makes you happy can boost your confidence. For example, if you enjoy painting, fixing cars, or other hobbies, whatever they may be—set aside time to pursue these fulfilling activities more often.

Do the Right Thing

When you do the right thing, you feel good about yourself. This can include helping others, being honest, and following your values and principles.

Do not Care What Others Think

When you stop caring about what others think, you free yourself from the pressure of trying to please everyone. It is important to remember that everyone has their own opinions, and you cannot control what others think of you.

Face Your Fears

Confronting your fears can be daunting, but it can also be liberating. Each time you confront and overcome a fear, you prove to yourself that you are capable of overcoming challenges. By taking small steps and gradually exposing yourself to your fears, you can build up your confidence and feel more in control.

Follow Through

When you follow through on your commitments, you prove to yourself that you are reliable and capable of achieving your goals. It also shows others that they can trust you, which can help build positive relationships and increase your confidence.

Get Sh*t Done

Accomplishing tasks, big or small, can help you feel productive and capable. Take time to celebrate your achievements, no matter how small they may be. Treat yourself to something you enjoy or give yourself a pat on the back for a job well done.

Polish Yourself Up

Taking care of your appearance is not just about looking good but also helps you feel good about yourself. When you feel confident in your appearance, it can help boost your self-esteem and make you feel more comfortable in your skin.

When you dress nicely, not only do you feel good about yourself, but it also reflects how you feel on the inside, projecting a positive image to others. You do not necessarily have to dress extravagantly, but dressing appropriately for the occasion and in a way that makes you feel confident and comfortable can go a long way in building your confidence.

Know When to Say "No"

Saying "no" when you need to can be empowering and help you establish healthy boundaries. It can also help you avoid overcommitting and feeling overwhelmed, which can negatively impact your confidence.

Live By Your Principles

Living by your principles can give you a sense of purpose and direction in life, which can increase your confidence in yourself and your decisions. It also helps you stay true to yourself and your values, which can help you feel more authentic and confident.

Monitor Your Progress

Tracking your progress toward your goals can help you stay motivated and focused on your achievements. Celebrating your successes, no matter how small, can help boost your confidence and give you a sense of accomplishment.

Practice Daily Gratitude

Practicing gratitude can help shift your mindset to a more positive one, which can increase your confidence and well-being. Focusing on what you have, rather than what you lack, can help you appreciate your strengths and accomplishments and feel more grateful for the opportunities in your life.

Practice Positive Self-Talk

Positive self-talk involves speaking kindly to yourself and replacing negative thoughts with positive affirmations. By practicing positive self-talk, you can improve your self-esteem and confidence and develop a more optimistic outlook on life.

Set Realistic Goals

Setting realistic goals can help you avoid setting yourself up for failure and instead focus on achievable targets. This can help you feel more confident in your abilities and increase your motivation to succeed.

Smile More Often

Smiling can help you feel happier and more positive, increasing your confidence and making you more approachable to others. It can also help reduce stress and anxiety, which can have a positive impact on your mental health and well-being.

Stand Up for Yourself and Stand Tall in the Face of Obstacles

Advocating for yourself can help you establish boundaries and feel more in control of your life. It can also help you build self-respect and confidence in your abilities and decisions. Standing tall under duress will make you more confident in your abilities and can allow others to take notice of your core strengths.

Stop Comparing Yourself to Others

Comparing yourself to others can be a confidence killer. Focus on your progress and accomplishments instead.

Surround Yourself With Positive People

Spending time with positive, supportive people can help you feel more confident and motivated. Seek out people who are optimistic and have a positive outlook on life. Avoid spending too much time with people who are negative, critical, or constantly bring you down.

Take Care of Your Body

Your physical health is closely linked to your mental health and confidence. Make sure you are taking care of your body by eating a healthy, balanced diet, getting regular exercise, and getting enough sleep. This can help you feel more energized, focused, and confident.

Think Long-Term

Building confidence is a process that takes time and effort. It is important to think long-term and have patience with yourself. Do not expect overnight results, but rather focus on making small, consistent changes over time that will lead to greater confidence and self-esteem.

Overall, boosting your confidence is a journey that requires self-reflection, patience, and consistent effort. By recognizing situations that affect your self-esteem, challenging negative thinking, adjusting your thoughts, doing more of what makes you happy, and taking care of your body, you can regain lost confidence and build a strong sense of self-worth.

Book 2: Magnetic Charm

Unleashing Your Inner Charisma
and Captivating Others

Kirsten Rae Evans

TABLE OF CONTENTS

Introduction 61

Chapter 1: Charismatic Individuals 63
    Archetypes of Charisma 63
    Powerful Elements of Charisma 65
    Characteristics of a Charismatic Person 67
    Benefits of Charisma 70

Chapter 2: Being Charismatic 73
    Building Charisma 73
    Traits of Charismatic People 76

Chapter 3: Ways to be More Charismatic 81

Introduction

Have you ever been drawn to someone who just exudes charisma? They seem to effortlessly command attention and inspire others to follow them. Charismatic individuals possess a magnetic quality that captivates and influences those around them. While some people may think that charisma is an innate talent, the truth is that it can be developed and cultivated over time.

In this book, we will explore the key traits and habits that can help you unleash your inner charisma and become a more captivating and influential communicator. Whether you are a leader, a salesperson, or simply want to make a stronger impression in your personal and professional life, mastering the art of charisma can help you achieve your goals and create deeper connections with others.

CHAPTER 1
CHARISMATIC INDIVIDUALS

Charisma is a quality that some people naturally radiate. While the capacity to be charismatic exists within all of us, some of us must play a more active role in cultivating and developing it. Once we develop high levels of authentic charisma, we can then utilize it to make lasting impressions on others.

It is a quality that is difficult to define, but when you see it, you know it. Charismatic individuals are those who have a magnetic charm that captivates others. Here, we will explore the different types of charisma, the powerful elements of charisma, the characteristics of a charismatic person, and the benefits of charisma.

Archetypes of Charisma

The archetypes of charismatic individuals that we will be exploring in this section include the following

- Authority
- Focus
- Kindness
- Visionary

Authority

Individuals that fit within this charismatic archetype are confident and self-assured. They have a natural ability to lead and influence others. They show gravitas, and their expertise and experience often command respect among their peers. These charismatic leaders know their stuff, and their credibility is never in doubt, but they do not ever wield their power over others or flaunt their credentials.

Not to be confused with the types of blind self-assuredness exhibited by narcissists and insecure individuals, true authority only comes from charismatic individuals who possess both integrity and the substantial backbone of having high levels of knowledge and competence—both in their area of expertise, as well as with relational, interpersonal skills that allow them to interact fairly and fluidly in their interactions with all types of people.

Focus

Individuals that fall under this charismatic archetype are fully present and focused on the person they are with. They make eye contact, listen attentively, and respond thoughtfully. Their body language speaks loudly, and they communicate that they care about the person they are with. This type of charisma helps build beneficial relationships, whether personal or professional.

This type of charisma is not to be confused with less genuine, pandering forms of flattery often exhibited by insecure individuals. This train is an expression of true empathy, in which people know that they are being heard and felt on an emotional level by the charismatic listener.

Kindness

Individuals classified under this charismatic archetype exude an aura of warmth and compassion. They are the most likable personalities, and people feel safe and taken care of around them. They are empathetic and genuine in their interactions, and they make others feel seen and heard. They are capable of building deep, long-lasting relationships and gaining loyalty through selfless actions.

Unlike people-pleasing insecure individuals, these genuine, kind, charismatic people do not compromise their boundaries or bend over backward to please others. Their strong sense of compassion and highly attuned and sensitive relational abilities allow them to communicate their own needs effectively. The warmth that they cast unto others is never to their own detriment; rather, it brings them great personal satisfaction and helps moderate and reinforces their own levels of happiness.

Visionary

Individuals under this charismatic archetype derive their attraction from the distinctiveness and bravery of the sometimes far-out or fantastic ideas. They are not afraid to challenge the status quo or do things that are contrary to established ways of doing and thinking. They are not necessarily extroverts, but they cast a powerful magnetic aura that draws people in through the power of their ideas.

Visionary types are capable of changing the world but never alone. They depend on others to create transformational new realities through cooperation and collaboration. By making others know that their own ideas are important and that they can participate in creating new realities, these types of charismatic individuals know the powers of teamwork and group ideation. They are confident, driven individuals who are capable of instilling ideas of hope and inspiration into others.

Powerful Elements of Charisma

The powerful elements of charisma that we will be exploring in this section include the following

- Power
- Presence
- Warmth

Power

Asserting power allows charismatic individuals to influence the world around them. By exuding leadership characteristics and channeling positive influence, they have the unique ability to shape reality and experience for themselves and others.

Knowing how to use power effectively and fairly is where things become complicated. It is important for charismatic, influential individuals to realize that power can become a dangerous tool when wielded incorrectly or towards nefarious means.

Presence

Having a presence makes others feel recognized and validated. By putting others at ease through outward empathetic gestures or unbridled, impassioned speech—charismatic individuals are able to build trust with their audience. This ultimately gives them the ability to convince people, priming them to receive messages and ideas. Charismatic individuals who've mastered the art of presence can build a familiar relationship with their audience members—even if they have never met them in person before.

Being aware of the ways in which charismatic presence can drive religious or political fervor is important to note. The most notorious dictators and cult leaders of all time were all well-versed in these tactics; it is important to note that they can be equally employed in ways that are detrimental to society as they can in ways that make a positive impact.

Warmth

If charismatic individuals are able to build personal relationships with people through their charismatic presence alone, what allows them to maintain these connections long-term is often through charismatic displays of warmth. In using this approach, speakers can connect with their audience long-term, on an emotional level. By showing that they are genuinely interested in others and are able to show empathy and compassion, charismatic individuals who employ warmth conveyance are not afraid to put their own vulnerabilities on the table. The effective use of warmth is often accomplished through sharing personal anecdotes or stories, which can help the speaker connect more deeply with their audience.

Also used to mitigate some of the inherent power imbalances sometimes encountered when looking at the addresser vs. addressee, the use of warmth is a powerful tool in the arsenal of any public speaker. Moreover, it can humanize individuals in positions of great power and can bridge social and ideological divides, aiding in delivering appeals and pleas in a way that cuts straight to the emotional core of the audience.

Characteristics of a Charismatic Person

The characteristics of charismatic people that we will be exploring in this section include the following

- Confidence
- Authenticity
- Enthusiasm
- Sense of humor

Confidence

Charismatic, confident individuals believe in themselves and their abilities. They are comfortable in their own skin and let others know it by radiating an aura of self-assurance everywhere they go. While some may think that confidence is about thinking that you are right and upholding your principles and beliefs—it is, in fact, more about the way you present yourself than it is about the ideas you hold.

Far from the kind of flaw-covering, often over-asserted "fake" self-assuredness often exhibited by narcissistic individuals with low levels of self-esteem—true confidence is never relied upon as a tool to mask our own deficits. Confidence is not stubbornness, it is a projection of our inner self-esteem and self-confidence that can serve as magnetic and influential when addressing our audience.

Authenticity

Charismatic, authentic individuals are genuine in presenting the angle that they are coming from and are honest in their interactions with others. These types of people are transparent about their priorities and agendas and never seek to conceal facets of their own personalities. They are never acting or simply going through the motions of life—they exhibit high levels of engagement because they are honest enough with themselves to not involve themselves in or get fixated on matters that are inconsequential. Authentic individuals are radically "themselves."

Authenticity is one of the more difficult-to-pin-down and one of the least easily attained qualities covered in this book. While some people are born with it, others spend decades finding themselves, eventually opening up paths to develop this essential core strength. To know oneself is the first step, and for some, this can take an entire lifetime. Given the fact that we all have such different internal psychological realities, there is no pre-prescribed way to acquire this trait.

Enthusiasm

Charismatic, enthusiastic individuals have a contagious enthusiasm for life. They are passionate about what they do and are able to inspire others to join in on their excitement. Enthusiastic people cultivate passions and wake up every day to the excitement these pursuits stir within them. They are experts at maintaining a positive attitude, but never in a fake way—their pragmatism and belief in positive outcomes allow them to take leaps of faith with ease and not get bogged down by negative feedback or results.

Though enthusiastic people make it look easy to maintain their engagement in the things they pursue with passion and vigor, their mastery of moderating their own levels of internal drive allows them to stay motivated, even in the face of significant obstacles. Taking breaks to recharge and top off their tanks periodically, then again propelling themselves forward with bursts of energy, enthusiastic people are an important asset in any group undertaking, public speaking included.

Sense of Humor

Charismatic, humorous individuals have a great sense of timing and delivery. They can instantly conjure up ice-breakers that serve as welcome interjections to awkward or uncomfortable introductory moments and can charm audiences with entertaining observations and musings. Most importantly, humorous people possess the ability to laugh at themselves, making them more relatable to their audience. Through the use of self-deprecating humor, they are able to set up genuine connections by building mutual empathy and understanding.

Like authenticity, developing a genuine sense of humor is not something that is attainable by all of us. The reality is some people are born better equipped to bring on laughter in a natural and unforced way. There is nothing more cringe than trying to force humor on others and bomb at it—so if you are not confident in your comedy skills, do not even give it a try. That said, one thing we *can* improve on is the level of joviality and levity we bring to the table when we are in public speaking situations. More indirect forms of humor, such as incorporating amusing graphics or other visual aids into our presentations, can help support the ease with which we deliver the spoken parts of public presentations.

Benefits of Charisma

The benefits of developing your levels of charisma that we will be exploring in this section include the following

- Increased confidence
- Improved relationships and networking
- Enhanced influence
- Increased self-confidence

Increased Confidence

Being charismatic can increase your confidence in yourself and your abilities. When you know that others are drawn to you and appreciate your unique qualities, it can help you feel more confident and self-assured. Charisma is a quality that tends to reflect on itself, and it can bring new opportunities and connections into your life.

Improved Relationships and Networking

The more charisma you are able to exhibit, the more charismatic people you will find yourself surrounded with—something which can spark new relationships and partnerships between yourself and others. Additionally, the more charisma you have, the more memorable your public speaking will be to your audience. Charisma can also boost your standing with higher-ups, increase your popularity and reputation among peers, and elevate your profile within your field.

Enhanced Influence

Once the profile-boosting powers of charisma have worked their magic, your world becomes suddenly open to a whole new set of possibilities set out before you. One of the most significant benefits of highly developed and realized charisma that you can use to your advantage is called enhanced influence.

Exerting enhanced influence simply means having the upper edge in terms of the power you now wield through your applied charisma. Enhanced influence allows you to influence and inspire others, allowing them to, in turn, rally around your original ideas and your unique point of view. This type of applied charisma can be applied to great effect in implementing new initiatives or projects at work, for example.

When you exhibit enhanced influence along with strong leadership skills, people are more likely to listen to what you have to say, follow your lead and feel inspired to join in on supporting your idea or cause.

Increased Self-Confidence

Charismatic individuals have a high level of self-confidence. They believe in themselves and their abilities, which makes them stand out from the crowd. They have a positive attitude towards life and always look at the brighter side of things. This confidence radiates from them, making them more attractive to others.

When you have self-confidence, you are more likely to take risks and try new things. You are not afraid of failure, and you are not deterred by setbacks. This can lead to greater success in both your personal and professional life.

What is Charisma?

Charisma is a powerful force that can make a significant impact on your life. By understanding the different types of charisma, the powerful elements that contribute to it, and the characteristics of charismatic individuals, you can develop your charisma and become more attractive and influential to others.

Charisma is not something that you are born with, but it is something that you can develop and cultivate over time. With practice and dedication, you can enhance your communication skills, build your confidence, and develop the traits associated with charismatic individuals.

Whether you want to be a better leader, a more persuasive communicator, or simply someone who is more attractive to others, developing your levels of charisma is a key step toward achieving these goals.

Chapter 2
Being Charismatic

Charisma is not just about attracting people and priming them to receive the powerful, impactful messages you want them to hear. Developing high levels of charisma can bring numerous broad benefits in addition to the more direct ones discussed in the previous chapter. Now, we will explore the various peripheral advantages of having a charismatic personality, how to cultivate charisma, and spot opportunities to gain from its benefits, as well as go over some common traits of charismatic people that can help you think about changing your habits and ingrained modes of thinking.

Building Charisma

Below are some reasons to build charisma.

Building Courage for Conviction

Charismatic people are not afraid to stand up for their beliefs and opinions. They have the courage to speak their mind, even in the face of opposition. This quality inspires others to do the same, creating a culture of openness and authenticity in their workplaces and communities.

You can practice this charismatic trait by taking bolder stances in the workplace in areas you have previously refrained from commenting on, whether it is on management structure or your benefits package. It may not make you popular with all the higher-ups, but it is certain to boost your profile among your peers and gain you respect.

Filling Gaps in Communication

Charismatic individuals are adept at reading people and understanding their needs. They have an uncanny ability to communicate in a way that resonates with others, making them feel heard and understood. This skill helps to bridge the gaps and divisions between people, facilitating better relationships and more effective collaboration.

One way you can start incorporating this charismatic trait is by asking more questions and showing more curiosity about what your peers are doing. By engaging them in discussions about their work and objectives and filling the gaps that often separate different workers and teams, you will have a better understanding of the full range of their experience and be better poised to support them.

Motivate and Inspiring Others

Charismatic individuals have a way of inspiring others to be their best selves. They possess the unique ability to motivate people to work towards their goals and achieve their dreams. This quality makes them excellent leaders who can bring out the best in their teams.

You do not have to be a manager yourself to motivate and inspire others. Simply showing up with a positive attitude and being a curious, inquisitive presence can do wonders toward setting a good example for others. Once people see you thriving, they will want to become closer to you and, in turn, more supportive of your ideas.

Promoting Collaboration and Team Building

Charismatic people know how to build relationships and bring people together. They are excellent at team building and collaboration, which is crucial in any organization. Their ability to create a positive and inclusive environment helps to foster creativity and drive innovation within their companies.

One way that you can start incorporating this charismatic trait is to organize team-building activities, such as group excursions or recreational activities. If you think this would be awkward, you can simply bring some snacks to work. Everyone likes snacks.

Standing Up for Others

Charismatic individuals have the power to use their platform as a champion for social causes. They are able to stand up for those who are marginalized or oppressed. They have a strong sense of justice and fairness and use their charisma to bring attention to causes that matter to them.

You can start exhibiting this charismatic trait by organizing a charity raffle, volunteer work, or other types of events that a broad range of your colleagues will agree is a worthy cause.

Making Life Better for Those Around You

Charismatic individuals have a contagious positive energy that can make life better for those around them. They have a way of lifting people's spirits and making them feel good about themselves.

You can start incorporating this charismatic trait by doling out compliments. The key is to ensure you are going about this respectfully and authentically—but yes! The power of a few genuine, kind words is really underestimated in today's world, but they will get you a long way.

Working Towards a Better Quality of Life

Charismatic individuals have a vision for their lives and the lives of those around them. They work towards creating a better future and improving the quality of life for themselves and others.

One way you can start incorporating this charismatic trait into your day-to-day routine is to think about the small improvements that *you* can make to yourself for the benefit of others. Though we commonly turn to external solutions when looking at ways to improve our quality of life, much of our experience comes down to human interaction.

By checking yourself and making sure that you have the ability to show up to things fully, you are doing a service to others, ensuring that interpersonal communication and interaction will go smoothly throughout the day.

Traits of Charismatic People

The traits of charismatic people are a subject that an entire book could be dedicated to exploring, but there are a few key ones that can help us on our journey towards developing the levels of confidence-boosting that will help us accomplish our goals and realize our dreams.

The traits of true charismatic individuals that we will be exploring in this section include:

- They possess inner depth and substance and err from the superficial.
- They act with maturity and have innate senses of duty and responsibility.
- They practice humility.
- They are effective verbal communicators and possess excellent listening skills

- They utilize body language to express themselves effectively.
- They exude confidence but are not ashamed of their vulnerabilities.

Possessing Inner Depth and Substance

True charismatic individuals possess inner substance and depth. They are almost never all talk, no action types. On the contrary, they tend to consistently live by their own high standard they set for themselves. They maintain a clear sense of purpose and direction in life and are deeply in touch with their own inner world.

Not to be mistaken with true charismatics, manipulative charismatics feign possessing inner depth and substance to fill the void with their own insecurity and latch on to vulnerable groups they can exploit.

Acting With Maturity

True charismatic individuals act maturely and responsibly. They are emotionally available and in tune with their own inner reality but are not easily swayed or influenced by emotional responses. They do not let their feelings cloud their judgment. They remain composed and level-headed, even in stressful situations.

Manipulative charismatics act infantile and are needy. They are in denial of the inner emotional realm and lash out at others due to their inability to process the complexities of their feelings. Their decisions are often impulsive or rash, and they are prone to outbursts of anger and fits of rage.

Being Humble

True charismatic individuals are humble and do not let their success get to their heads. They are grounded and have a trail cut out for themselves, marked with goals and milestones along the way. The trail they blaze is characterized by a deep sense of purpose. They know that they are not perfect and are always willing to learn and grow.

Manipulative charismatics are egotistical and obsessed with success and personal gain. They are often messy and disorganized, meandering a wayward path that often jumps from one thing, or another based on trends or spotted opportunities rather than core convictions and deep beliefs. They often look foolish because they think they are perfect, while it is clear to others that they are not.

Maintaining Great Communication Skills

True charismatic individuals are excellent communicators. They know how to articulate their thoughts and ideas in ways that are easy to understand. They are also good at active listening and paying attention to what others have to say.

Manipulative charismatic individuals use catchphrases and sloganeering as substitutes for thoughtful discourse. They are proficient at honing their messages to reach the masses and delivering them in palatable ways. They have difficulties listening to outside voices and often ignore the thoughts and opinions of others.

Utilizing Body Language Effectively

True charismatic individuals have a commanding presence and display excellent body language, which makes their audience feel connected to them. They stand tall, speak clearly, and maintain eye contact, exuding confidence and charisma. Their audience remains engaged and attentive and is open to taking inspiration and new ideas.

Manipulative charismatics use choreographed hand gestures and deliver performative, sometimes barked-out routines that whip their audiences into an impassioned frenzy. With an emphasis on spectacle and power, they are highly effective in rallying numbers, but they often forfeit individual connection with the audience for the mass effect of crowd dynamics.

How to Exude Confidence While Still Being Vulnerable and Open

True charismatic individuals radiate confidence and self-assuredness. They know who they are and what they stand for, and they are not afraid to show it. They are assertive but know how to show their vulnerability. Their audience is drawn to them and their message because their more humble, humanistic qualities are laid out for all to see.

Manipulative charismatics radiate authority, power, and unanimity. They have a well-defined image of themselves they wish to project, and they will go to lengths to protect it. They are assertive and forceful and err from showing the vulnerability of any kind. Their audience is drawn to them and their message because it feels powerful and cathartic.

To Sum Things Up

The benefits of developing charisma go far beyond simply being likable. A charismatic person can positively impact their personal and professional lives in numerous ways, including increased confidence, better communication skills, stronger relationships, and enhanced leadership abilities. By understanding the different types and powerful elements of charisma and working to develop key characteristics such as substance, maturity, humility, and strong communication and listening skills, anyone can unleash their inner charisma and captivate others. So whether you are looking to boost your career, enhance your personal relationships, or simply become a more confident and influential individual, developing charisma is a valuable skill to cultivate.

CHAPTER 3
WAYS TO BE MORE CHARISMATIC

Are you wondering how you can improve your charisma and make a positive impact on those around you, even if you are naturally a more shy, introverted, or reserved person? The good news is that you do not have to be born with a magnetic personality to start incorporating charismatic traits into your daily interactions with the people around you.

Fortunately, charisma *is* something that can be actively developed and cultivated. In this chapter, we will explore practical and actionable ways to express your charismatic personality and become a more engaging and likable person.

The strategies for strengthening and reinforcing your levels of charisma that we will be exploring in this section include

- Using rhetorical questions to drive engagement and participation.
- Embracing your vulnerability as an appeal to your audience.
- Being attuned to and embracing your flaws.
- Finding mutuality between yourself and your audience.
- Speaking with your hands is an effective tool for communication.
- Being a responsive, engaged listener.

- Making eye contact with your audience.
- Practicing empathy and emotional availability.
- Setting high goals for yourself is a way to draw others in.
- Sharing stories and personal anecdotes as a way of relating to people.
- Using body language to entice and convince your audience.
- Addressing people on a one-to-one personal level.
- Using vocabulary that would not alienate or confuse your audience.

Pose Rhetorical Questions to Your Audience

Asking rhetorical questions can help you keep your audience engaged and encourage them to think more critically. Rhetorical questions are questions that do not require an answer but rather serve to make a point or emphasize a particular idea. For example, instead of saying, "I have a great idea," try saying, "What if I told you I had a great idea?" This engages your listener and encourages them to consider what you are saying in a more participatory and engaging way.

Embrace Vulnerability

Vulnerability is not a weakness but rather a strength that allows you to connect with others on a deeper level. Sharing your personal vulnerabilities can make you more relatable and approachable to others. It can also help others open up and feel comfortable sharing their own vulnerabilities with you.

For example, sharing a personal story of a struggle you faced and how you overcame it can inspire and encourage others to do the same. In fact, rather than making you feel ashamed or lesser, opening up about your vulnerabilities can help form lasting connections between yourself and your audience members.

Embrace Your Flaws

No one is perfect. Pretending to be a well-put-together, polished, and presentable person at all times can come across as insincere or unrelatable. Let people know you are human and that it is unrealistic to be "on" at all moments. We all need downtime and moments where we focus on our inner world rather than how we outwardly present ourselves to the world. Do not be afraid to show other parts of this side of you, even in professional settings. Let people know how human you are.

You will find that embracing your flaws and imperfections and not being afraid to share them with others can make you more relatable and likable. Acknowledge your weaknesses and show that you are willing to learn and grow from them. For example, dropping anecdotes about silly mistakes you have made will be something your audience can connect with.

While it may be embarrassing at first to talk about these things in front of a crowd, you will soon find out through people's reactions that the more you reveal your flaws and weaknesses, the more engaged and drawn into what you are saying, your audience will become.

Find Mutuality

Mutuality refers to finding common ground with your audience and showing them that you are on the same page. When you can connect with someone on a shared experience or interest, it can help to build rapport and establish a connection.

For example, if you meet someone for the first time, find out what you have in common and use that as a starting point for conversation. In this same way, when speaking in front of a group of people, you can also use this technique to bridge the gaps between yourself and your audience.

One way you can accomplish this is by making your speech participatory, by asking engaging non-rhetorical questions or prompts and then letting your audience know that you feel similarly to the way they do. By validating their points of view, you have gained a valuable inroad that will allow the proceeding themes you bring up in your speech to be more impactful on them.

Keep Your Hands in View and Use Them to Help You Speak

Using hand gestures while you speak can help to emphasize your points and make your presentation more engaging. Keeping your hands in view can also make you appear more open and approachable. For example, you can use your hands to show the size or shape of something you are describing or make a more emphatic point.

You do not want to look like you are conducting an orchestra or anything, but the effective use of hand gestures can really enhance your speeches and help emphasize key moments that will support driving in your key points. Certain hand gestures can also convey a range of different moods and feelings, such as openness, sincerity, and gratefulness. If you are able to incorporate these types of gestures into your speech, you will be able to better convince your audience.

Listen Wholeheartedly

Genuinely listening to someone is a powerful way to show that you care and build a deeper connection. When someone else is speaking, give them your full attention and show that you are interested in what they have to say. Avoid interrupting or rushing the conversation. For example, if someone shares a story, give them the space and time to finish without interrupting or changing the subject.

If part of engaging your audience during your speech involves asking non-rhetorical questions and prompts, or if it includes a Q&A session, use body language cues to let your audience members know you are listening to them while they are speaking. When addressing questions from audience members, try to open your response with a piece of positive feedback such as: "great question," or "what an interesting observation," before proceeding with the rest of your response.

Look People in Their Beautiful Eyes

Maintaining eye contact can help establish trust and connection with your audience, and it shows that you are confident, present, and engaged in the conversation. When you are speaking to someone directly, it can be easier than when you are addressing a crowd. With one-on-one conversations, all you need to do is look the person in the eyes while making sure that your gaze is warm and inviting. But how do you deal with this when speaking in front of an audience?

When speaking in front of a group of people, you can make eye contact with individual audience members, making them feel more engaged in the flow of your speech and more involved in the subject matter being discussed. This can take some practice, but once you get the hang of it, you will see what a difference it can make.

Practice Listening to Other People's Emotions

One thing you will notice about charismatic people is that not only are they good at listening to the details of what people say, but they also excel at picking up on the emotions behind the words. They pay attention to the tone, body language, and facial expressions of others to get a sense of how they are feeling.

You can practice this by making an extra effort to show empathy and understanding by acknowledging the emotions of others and responding to them with sensitivity and care. You will find that this essential practice is not just relegated to your personal life and in dealing with your friends, family members, and significant others. More and more, people are expected to bring emotional availability to the workplace.

While you should not expect to receive additional compensation for this additional labor that is expected of you—it is important to recognize it is becoming a norm in corporate contexts. Soft skills are ever more important in these spaces, so if you are feeling out of practice or over your head when it comes to being emotionally available toward others, it may be time to brush up on your skills in this crucial area of interpersonal communication.

Set High Goals and Express Confidence That You Can Achieve Them

Another trait that high-performing charismatic people often exhibit is that they are goal-oriented and confident in their abilities to achieve their long-term strategic objectives. Their expression of confidence in reaching their objectives does not stem from blind faith or hope; rather, it comes from their deep knowledge that they would not get derailed by the obstacles they will surely have to confront along the way. Only through accepting the inevitability of these hiccups can they look forward without fear.

One way you can start incorporating this into your approach to life, and something which you can start getting results from right away, is to start setting more ambitious goals for yourself. Start sharing your goals with others more often and express your confidence in your ability to achieve your goals. For example, instead of saying "I hope, you can say "I will." or "I am going to" This kind of language and mindset communicates to others that you are proactive and confident in your abilities to achieve your goals. Becoming more resilient is another part of it. The way we become more resilient is often through failure and through rolling with the punches that life throws at us. Having a positive, forward-looking attitude while confronting the problems of the present is key in working towards developing high-performance charismatic traits and eventually reaching your goals.

Share Stories and Anecdotes

People love stories, and sharing personal anecdotes is a great way to connect with others and show your personality. Sharing stories can also make you more relatable and help others understand where you are coming from. "Against the odds" narratives are great for crafting compelling assertions that highlight your confidence and skills. Personal stories with humorous content help keep your audience engaged and open them up to having new ideas or concepts introduced to them. Anecdotes about your family life help humanize you and remind audience members of their own families, creating shared connections.

You can start incorporating these techniques more by using more examples and metaphors when explaining your ideas. Think about how the projects you work on, and ideas you come up with relate to your origin story, family life, and place in society. Once you start making these connections more often, the possibilities for creating relatable anecdotes and stories that reinforce your ideas and your vision are endless.

Use Body Language Effectively

Smiling is one of the simplest yet most effective ways to show your charisma. A genuine smile can make you appear more approachable, friendly, and confident. Start showing more expression on your face in general. Your facial expressions can communicate a lot about how you are feeling and what you are thinking. You can increase your charisma and connection with others by consciously using your facial expressions to match the emotion you are trying to convey.

When it is others' turn to speak, make sure you are using body language that signals to them that you are engaged in what they are saying. Techniques such as leaning forward and taking notes while others are speaking can signal that you are interested in what they are saying and that their dialogue is generating new ideas in your mind. You can also make eye contact with them while they are speaking to let them know you are actively listening.

Use Your Listener's Name

Addressing members of your audience by name helps create a sense of familiarity and build a more personal connection with them. When you do use the technique of calling out audience members by name, be careful not to overuse it, as this can start to come across as insincere or manipulative. You do not want to sound like a used car salesperson but rather like a competent professional. Especially when delivering speeches based on pitching new ideas, make sure you do not sound like a schlocky infomercial.

Name-dropping during public speeches can also be a great tool, as it can allow you to highlight the hard work of others present, such as your manager or team members. This can help to boost the profiles of your peers while reinforcing your credibility.

Use Words People Can Relate To

Using complex jargon or technical language can alienate others and make it difficult to connect. Instead, try to use language that is relatable and easy to understand. This can make it easier for others to engage with you on these topics after you speak on them and can also help to establish a rapport between you and your audience while you are speaking.

It is especially important to consider who your audience is when considering the vocabulary you use. While you do not want to talk down to people or oversimplify ideas—you also do not want to overcomplicate things. It is about striking the right balance between being accessible and effectively transmitting the intricacies and complexities of your subject matter.

How to Become More Charismatic Summed Up

Charisma is not something that you are necessarily born with; it can be developed through conscious effort and practice. By applying the techniques outlined here, you can begin to express your charismatic personality and connect more effectively with others. Remember that being charismatic is not about being fake or insincere but rather about being confident, genuine, and empathetic. With practice and patience, anyone can become more charismatic and successful in their personal and professional lives.

Book 3: The Art of Words

Mastering Speech Preparation for
Impactful Communication

Kirsten Rae Evans

TABLE OF CONTENTS

Introduction 95

Chapter 1: Speech Preparation Essentials **97**
    The Four Types of Public Speaking 97
    Causes of Bad Communication 102

Chapter 2: The Benefits of Good Public Speaking **111**
    Benefits of Good Public Speaking Skills 112

Chapter 3: Tips to Improve Your Public Speaking **121**

Introduction

The words we use and how we use them can greatly impact our ability to communicate effectively. Whether you are giving a presentation, delivering a speech, or engaging in a casual conversation, preparing your words and delivery can make all the difference. In this book, we will explore the art of words and speech preparation, discussing strategies and techniques to help you communicate with impact and clarity. From understanding your audience to crafting compelling messages, we will cover key elements of effective communication and equip you with the tools you need to master the art of words.

Chapter 1
Speech Preparation Essentials

Public speaking is an essential skill that can help individuals communicate effectively, influence others, and achieve their goals. However, it is also a complex art that needs to be learned and practiced. In this chapter, we will explore the speech preparation essentials that can help you eliminate the habits that can result in bad communication and become a more effective public speaker.

Before you start learning about these techniques, however, it is important to understand the different types of public speaking out there. Each type of public speech involves different goals and is judged upon different sets of criteria in terms of its effectiveness.

The Four Types of Public Speaking

There are four main types of public speaking, each with its own set of requirements and challenges. In this section, we will be running through the goals and steps for each type of public speaking scenario, along with some pointers that can help prepare for your public speaking endeavors.

The types of public speaking that we will be exploring in this section include

- Ceremonial speaking
- Demonstrative speaking
- Informative speaking
- Persuasive speaking

Ceremonial Speaking

(i.e., graduation speech, commencement addresses, wedding toast, business milestones, and summits)

Goals

- To confer accolades and to acknowledge achievement
- To put the achievements being highlighted into context (highlighting their social impact and benefits)
- To toast and celebrate the people being acknowledged

Steps

1. Thank your audience.
2. Emphasize that this is a special day.
3. Highlight the factors behind the occasion that is brought everyone together.
4. Speak about your experience, accomplishments, and the challenges that brought you there, and tie them in with the accomplishments being highlighted. (when appropriate—such as in a graduation speech or commencement address)
5. Speak about the benefits and gains realized by the people being acknowledged.
6. Speak about the future prospects of the people being acknowledged.
7. Let everybody know that it is time to celebrate.

Pointers

- Add personal touches to your speech to make it more engaging and memorable.
- Incorporate humor when appropriate to hold your audience's engagement.
- Stay mindful of the main message to avoid going off-topic.
- Practice brevity to avoid losing your audience's interest.

Demonstrative Speaking

(i.e., hard science and math lectures, informative presentations, engineering and manufacturing demonstrations, technical and process-based subject matter)

Goals

- To confer specific knowledge
- To demonstrate specific, concrete concepts and ideas

Steps

1. Introduce yourself and let the audience know who you are and what your credentials are (when appropriate).
2. Pose a rhetorical question that grabs your audience's interest.
3. Explain the step-by-step processes defining your presentation's main subject matter.
4. Talk about any challenges encountered along the way in personal terms that will allow your audience to feel connected to you.
5. Summarize the material covered and tell the audience that you have appreciated their attentiveness.
6. Thank the audience for their time and open up the discussion to field any questions they may have (when relevant).

Pointers

- Develop a deep technical knowledge of the subject matter before speaking on it so you can communicate your thoughts and opinions effectively.
- Use visual aids, such as diagrams or charts, to enhance your presentation.
- Consider engaging your audience with interactive elements, such as hands-on demonstrations or non-rhetorical questioning, that allow them to participate while you are presenting.

Informative Speaking

(i.e., general presentations, lectures, generalized and global, or specific non-technical subject matter)

Goals

- To confer generalized and specific ideas and subject matter
- To encourage your audience to actively engage with and think about the topics being discussed on a deep level

Steps

1. Introduce yourself and let the audience know who you are and what your credentials are (when appropriate).
2. Pose a rhetorical question that grabs your audience's interest.
3. Start by telling a story or anecdote, either something shocking or exciting about the subject matter at hand (fun fact) or something about your personal experience that relates back to the subject matter.
4. Tell your audience about the subject matter, making sure to use devices such as analogy to make it relatable to them.

5. Pose non-rhetorical questions to drive audience participation and engagement.
6. Summarize the concepts covered.
7. Ask if there are any questions and be available to field them.

Pointers

- Build credibility by using research and statistics to support your points.
- Cultivate leadership skills by establishing yourself as an authority on the subject matter.
- Facilitate conversation by asking questions and actively listening to your audience.

Persuasive Speaking

(i.e., thesis statements, business presentations, sales pitches, etc.)

Goals

- To introduce your ideas to your audience
- To convince the audience of the merits of your ideas
- To gain the support of your audience

Steps

1. Introduce yourself, and sincerely thank your audience for being there to hear what you are about to say.
2. Give the audience some insight into your journey: What is the story behind you being there today? What are your motivations, and what is the driving force behind the material you are presenting?
3. Use personal anecdotes to warm the crowd up to see you as a person rather than as a pitchman.

4. Pose a problem. This could be posed as a rhetorical question or could take the form of an anecdote.
5. Tell your audience that there is a solution to the problem, a solution that you have been laboring over tirelessly.
6. Introduce the main crux of your argument, breaking down the points of your argument into clearly structured talking points.
7. Make an appeal to your audience, letting them know how your idea can serve as a solution to the problem you previously identified.
8. Summarize the main benefits of your idea and thank your audience for their time.

Pointers

- Learn to craft your message to appeal to your audience's emotions, values, and interests.
- Modulate your tone of voice to convey confidence and enthusiasm.
- Work on your body language to enhance your message and establish trust with your audience.

Causes of Bad Communication

Bad, ineffective communication can have many causes; some of which are within our control and others we have no control over. In this section, we will be running through some of the most common causes of bad communication:

Culture Clashes

Cultural norms and values differences can sometimes lead to misunderstandings or even miscommunications. Even if you are working exclusively with people from a similar background as you, there are always bound to be points of difference that sometimes can become points of contention. The important thing to be mindful of here is that everyone deserves your respect, despite cultural differences. If you take this even-handed diplomatic approach, you are bound to be respected by all of your peers, regardless of their backgrounds.

In today's workplace, the word "culture" is often thrown around to describe the beliefs, values, and practices that companies expect their employees to uphold. It is important to recognize that companies are made up of people, and not everyone will fit neatly into this kind of mold. Culture clashes can arise when there are unrealistic expectations that can demoralize employees and make them feel like just a cog in the wheel of a greater system which they have no control over. Try to be lenient of others and not judge them for failure to "fit in," it may just be that they feel pushed to the fringes by whatever dominant ideas are at play in the workplace.

Distance and Time Zones

The nature of today's global workforce means that more than ever, you are likely to collaborate with a diverse pool of people who span multiple time zones. The geographic and cultural gaps that stem from this reality are worth considering if you want to be an effective communicator across the board. Learning how to respect different cultural backgrounds while adapting to different communication styles is an important undertaking.

While physical distance and time differences make communication more challenging—the widespread use of technology allows us to bridge the gap and facilitate communication. This does not mean we do not have to take active roles in mitigating the inherent cultural gaps and disparities that still exist despite our digital connections. Be sensitive and polite towards whomever you are communicating with, regardless of background or position.

Ego Check

Ego can lead to poor listening skills and a lack of empathy. In dynamic, collaborative environments, there is little room for people with huge egos, at least not within the general ranks. While corporate CEOs have been shown to exhibit high levels of psychopathy by some studies (Babiak et al., 2010), demonstrating these types of characteristics does not bode well for the majority of workers.

An over-inflated ego can lead to profound levels of poor communication and the creation of a toxic work environment. Having the poor listening skills that often accompany having an over-inflated ego is a trait that makes us more likely to come across as ineffective speakers, and it is one we have to be aware of. For some, it is something that needs to be actively combatted.

One way we can be more mindful of this is to pay attention to and try to hone our active listening skills better. We can do this by using our body language to show that we are attentive and by asking thoughtful questions that signal the fact we have a genuine interest in others' perspectives. The next time you are struggling with communication issues at work, you may want to consider checking your ego.

Fragmented or Insufficient Knowledge

Lack of knowledge or information can lead to misunderstandings and miscommunications in the workplace and in other areas of life. You can work on this by trying never to jump to conclusions until all the facts are in place and by being less judgmental in general. While we often have the urge to be the first to speak or have the answers and solutions to a problem at hand, if our presumptions are based on fragmented or insufficient knowledge, we are only doing ourselves a disservice.

In public speaking, if we feign competence or knowledge in a subject, we are lying not only to ourselves but to a group of people, the results of which can be somewhat embarrassing. Once it becomes clear that we have no idea what we are talking about but rather are postulating based on false pretenses, the effectiveness of our speech, even if well-prepared and delivered with pizzazz, can quickly disintegrate. Do your research, ask questions, and seek clarification *before* you go public with facts that might be challenged. It will save you a lot of grief later down the line.

Ignorance and Inappropriateness

Ignorance about sensitive cultural or social issues can lead to insensitive or offensive communication. The kind of vocabulary that is permitted in the workplace has changed a lot over the past few decades. If you have been around long enough to remember the Mad Men era of office culture, you are probably retired by now, but if you are a little younger than that and still working—it may be time for a refresh or a crash course in cultural appropriateness.

Educate yourself about current events and cultural trends. You do not have to go all "woke" or become excessively aware of every social issue or sensitivity to understand the fundamentals of what is acceptable today. For example, referring to Women as "Ladies" is frowned upon these days, and commenting on a co-worker's physical appearance can be treated as a serious HR issue. If you are an experienced older worker who's feeling over their head in the rules of the new workplace, you can always rely on a younger colleague to fill you in. This way, you would not embarrass yourself when it comes time to speak publicly in front of an ever-younger audience at your place of work.

Lack of trust

A lack of trust can lead to suspicion and defensive communication. Building positive, trusting relationships among your teammates and colleagues is an essential part of maintaining your ability to deliver effective public speeches. If you are the type of person who goes behind peoples' backs to get things done or who constantly makes promises that go unfulfilled, you may be putting your reputation on the line in more ways than you know. What happens is the less and less trust others have in you—the less responsive they will be to the messages you deliver when it comes time to engage in public speaking.

You can cement trust in others by practicing transparency, honesty, and open communication with higher-ups as well as with your peers. Being accountable, reliable, and owning up to your mistakes will also go a long way in reinforcing your trustworthiness. Your everyday body language as well can signal to others that you have nothing to hide and that you act transparently. Some people cross their arms habitually, but it can signal to others that you are concealing something. Also, be aware that your facial expressions can come into play. If your eyes are often downcast, it may signal to others that you are holding things back.

Politics

Politics can create a hostile environment that discourages open communication. While it is best to avoid political discussions entirely in certain contexts, it is considered the norm in some places of work. It is of the utmost importance to gauge those around you and their comfort with certain topics before breaching the surface on any potentially sensitive or contentious matters.

If you do find yourself in an environment where political discussion is open, and you happen to get into a disagreement with someone, there are a few steps to take to make sure you do not offend anyone. Focus on the issues at hand and avoid personal attacks or negative language. Be mindful of the tone of your voice so as to not come off as rude or belligerent. Also, letting your debate partner politely know that you respect their opinion, even though it is different from yours, can go a long way.

Aside from outwardly-focused political discussion, there can be a whole number of other issues that arise from talking about intraorganizational politics. An entire book in itself could be written about the politics of the office, so I am not going into the details here. But like with any sensitive discussions in the workplace, discussions of office politics are best carried out with diplomacy and using our well-honed listening skills to let others know that they are heard and to remain open to different ideas rather than being judgmental.

Power and Hierarchy

Power imbalances between the speaker and the audience can lead to one-sided or unfair communication. If you are in a position of power, and addressing your subordinates, make sure to be aware of the inherent discrepancies in power between yourself and your audience and that you craft your message to address this reality. The nature of this relationship could mean that your audience may feel compelled to accept your ideas simply because you wield power over them. This is something you want to avoid, as it may lead to ineffective, bad communication.

While it seems like this dynamic could be leveraged to your advantage, it can actually make your audience pay less attention to the content of your message. This puzzling conundrum can be attributed to the possibility that your audience may be paying more attention to your status and the way in which you deliver your message than the words themselves. If you are mindful of power dynamics, you can strive to achieve more open, honest, and effective communication with your subordinates.

Preconceived Notions and Judgments:

Preconceived notions and judgments can lead to biased or inaccurate communication. If you are coming at a problem thinking that you have already found the solution, and your reasoning is based on preconceived ideas—your communication may be ineffective. Failure to see where the true issues lie can be attributed to this misguided approach.

Be open-minded and willing to consider alternative perspectives. When appropriate, you can present multiple points-of-view, and multiple solutions to problems. This way, you can cover all the bases and explore the issues at hand from multiple angles. Sometimes the reason why communication is ineffective is because it takes too reductive an approach. Once you acknowledge the complexities of problems and ideas in a way that discards your preconceived notions, you will be able to craft messages that are thoughtful and will stick with your audience. You can do this by applying evidence-based approaches to analyzing information rather than making judgments based on your opinions.

Inefficiency of Words

Talking too much can be a sign of insecurity, and this technique is often used to mask the fact that you do not actually have something to say. It can also signal to your audience that you are desperately reaching for the right way to explain things and that you have not put much thought into preparing your speech in a well-crafted, meaningful, and effective format.

The inefficiency of words can also come from trying to sound smart. Often, people equate the volume of words spoken with the depth of content; however, this is often not the case. When presenting, the words you use should be rich and descriptive but also stay focused on the main point. Complex ideas take time to hash out, but there should be an emphasis on clarity and ease of understanding. Focus not just on delivering your words with a purpose but also on making sure that each word you choose has a purpose. If you are able to accomplish word efficiency while effectively communicating complex ideas, you will avoid one of the most common pitfalls of bad communication.

Ulterior Motives

Hidden agendas or ulterior motives can lead to distrust and misunderstanding. An essential part of delivering effective, poignant messages to your audience is being transparent and honest about your intentions and motivations. If you are coming to a public speaking event with an ulterior motive or attempting to veil one thing as another, the core message of the words you are delivering could be compromised by the fact that you are not being honest with your audience.

While in the short-run, your cover-up may be accepted by your audience and may even lead to results, the negative long-term ramifications could end up compromising your reputability. One way you can avoid this is by being upfront with your audience and disclosing any conflicts of interest you may have. You can also incorporate more participatory elements into your speech that will build trust between yourself and your audience and signal to them that you do not have ulterior motives.

To Sum Things Up

Speech preparation is essential for effective communication. By understanding the different types of public speaking and the causes of bad communication, you can improve your skills and become a more confident and influential public speaker.

Chapter 2
The Benefits of Good Public Speaking

Effective communication is an essential skill that is beneficial in all aspects of life. Let's discuss the numerous advantages of having strong public speaking skills.

The benefits of obtaining high-level effective communication skills that we will be exploring in this section include:

- They allow you to communicate in a way that conveys leadership and goal-oriented ideas.
- They boost your confidence through the communication feedback loop.
- They aid you in building trust among your peers and colleagues.
- They can help you advance your career.
- They can help you build better relationships in your personal and business life.
- They can boost the magnitude and scope of your ideas and their impact on the world.
- They can improve your critical thinking skills through effective high-level implementation of communication strategies.
- They can help you become a better listener by building more experience with effective communication.
- They can lead to personal and career development.

- They can help you expand your network of colleagues or business contacts and increase your reliability and standing among them.
- They can help you elevate your personal brand and public perception.
- They can help you increase customer and client engagement in business ventures.
- They can help you increase innovation within your team or department at work.
- They can reinforce your confidence and grow your personal satisfaction across all facets of life.
- They can improve your capacity for conflict mitigation.
- They can enhance your troubleshooting skills.
- They can give your life and work a sense of direction.
- They can help you clarify your thoughts and thought processes.

Benefits of Good Public Speaking Skills

Leadership Building

Public speaking skills are critical for leadership, as they help to motivate and inspire people, resulting in better team management. Acquiring these skills will give you the tools you need to become a natural leader. People will turn to you for advice on important matters once they have seen you flex your public speaking abilities.

Boosting Confidence

Good public speaking skills improve one's self-esteem, self-image, and self-worth. The feedback you will receive from your audience once you put your newly-acquired public speaking skills to the test can help further reinforce the confidence you have already worked so hard on cementing. Feeling like you have a positive impact on the lives of others can also help boost your internal levels of confidence and will make you more likely to reach out to others in the future.

Building Trust

Effective public speaking communication helps build trust among individuals, leading them to form more substantial partnerships in the future. Once you have the levels of trust that your newly-acquired public speaking abilities will bring, a whole world of new opportunities can open up before you. Increased trust in you can lead to new responsibilities and promotions.

Career Advancement

Public speaking skills are essential for career advancement, as they enable individuals to express their ideas and opinions with clarity and conviction. Career advancement does not just mean getting promoted to a more respected and better-compensated position. It could also mean branching out into new fields or new lines of work. Having good public speaking skills could put you on a track that will allow you to successfully change careers or even start your business.

Creating Better Relationships

The ability to communicate effectively creates better relationships, leading to a more harmonious and productive personal and professional life. Once you are able to assert yourself with purpose and conviction, others will be inspired to do the same in your presence. This sympathetic mutual exchange can help improve the dynamics of preexisting relationships, as well as bring new ones into your life.

Improving Day-to-Day Communication Skills

Public speaking skills improve communication, enabling individuals to express their thoughts, ideas, and emotions with clarity and confidence. You can apply your newly-acquired public speaking skills to small groups and even to one-on-one conversations. You will find that the skills that make a great public speaker can make you an effective communicator across all facets of your life.

Enhancing Critical Thinking Skills

Good public speaking skills require individuals to synthesize information effectively and format it into compelling, digestible blocks of content. Through practice and building more experience with public speaking engagements, you will be able to apply these skills gained towards your approach to other areas of your life which require critical thinking and deep analysis. You will see a marked improvement in your performance on a wide range of tasks that require your applied mental effort.

Helping You Become a Better Listener

Developing good public speaking skills can help you listen more actively, leading to better communication, mutual understanding, and fewer conflicts and misunderstandings. The newfound diplomatic and negotiation skills that this can bring can open up a whole world of new possibilities for you. You will find yourself managing all types of social situations with ease and will become a relied-upon asset at work and at home.

Aiding in Personal Development

Public speaking skills help individuals to develop personally by increasing self-awareness, self-confidence, and self-expression. When we learn how to express ourselves in front of groups, we can gain a better sense of ourselves—which helps hone our purpose and direction in life. By allowing ourselves to be vulnerable and powerful simultaneously in front of others, we can increase our capacity for self-expression in all different ways. Possessing high levels of self-awareness is an important driving factor in how we come off to others and how we identify ourselves within our communities and workplaces. Developing good public speaking skills can aid in building and reinforcing these essential qualities, which are crucial to personal development.

Improving Networking Opportunities

Public speaking skills enable individuals to connect with others, leading to better networking opportunities and career growth. The fact that many high-profile public speaking engagements are recorded these days means that you can even share your public speaking successes on platforms like LinkedIn and YouTube. You may find that publishing your public speaking engagements (when permitted) can increase your opportunities for networking with others in your industry.

In the case of private-public speaking engagements, such as at work—these applied demonstrations of your talent can increase your networking opportunities within your company. If your company permits it, you may be able to share your speeches with your colleagues whom you do not have direct experience working with on internal messaging apps like Slack.

Improving Your Personal Brand and Public Image

Public speaking skills are crucial in creating a positive impression in the minds of others, leading to a stronger public perception. This can give you greater exposure and can thereby provide you with access to more opportunities. Developing a personal brand is important these days, even for workers with well-established careers. Cultivating a positive, reliable image with outsiders by applying your public speaking abilities can become a meaningful asset. Name recognition in your field is priceless, even if you are not seeking a new job.

Increasing Audience Engagement

Public speaking skills are essential in driving engagement and in keeping people interested in the work you are doing and the ideas you have. Once you have developed and applied the skills necessary to be a great public speaker, it is likely that you will start seeing your inbox fill up. The more influential your ideas become, the more people will start reaching out to you, seeking to connect their ideas with yours through collaborations or new ventures. Driving engagement is a valuable tool for influencers and entrepreneurs, but it can also be useful to you if you work within a company. Keeping your colleagues engaged will help uphold the reputation you have already built among them.

Increasing Innovation

Public speaking skills encourage creativity and innovation, leading to better problem-solving and new ideas. This goes hand and hand with improving critical thinking and analytical skills brought on through the conscious efforts you have made to improve your public speaking.

With your newly-acquired public speaking skills, you will be able to use your influential powers to drive change and innovation within your team at work or within your company as a whole by making compelling proposals to inspire those around you. Your thoughtful and well-articulated ideas can become the kindling to sparks of innovation and success if you learn how to make sure they reach the right people.

Increasing Life Satisfaction

Good public speaking skills lead to more security and success in your career, higher levels of self-esteem, and increased levels of overall life satisfaction. Being able to speak out and express your ideas clearly can make you feel more connected to the community you live in and in greater society. Cultivating and reinforcing these skills can give you a higher standing within your community and make you a trusted voice in local politics or organizing efforts.

The ability to lead and help others is a noble one. And if you do take on new responsibilities that build on your experience with public speaking, you can use these positions as a chance to advocate for improvements and changes. This newfound ability can create a positive feedback loop, where your continued good deeds and advocacy efforts, through utilizing your public speaking skills, can elevate your life satisfaction levels to heights previously unknown.

Mitigating Intrapersonal and Intragroup Conflicts

Having good public speaking skills can help resolve intrapersonal conflicts and fractured group dynamics by rallying the audience towards common causes and also by empowering them to communicate their thoughts, opinions, and feelings clearly and respectfully. They can increase our ability to foster an atmosphere of mutual understanding and can make us well-poised to take on roles that involve mediation and conflict resolution. These abilities can be useful at work and also at home.

Once you have developed good public speaking skills, you will find that people will turn to you for guidance on difficult issues, making your skills more in demand and needed. The ability to bring people together is perhaps one of the greatest benefits of developing good public speaking skills. A good public speaker has the ability to dissolve tension between groups and individuals and break through boundaries of difference toward inclusion. An excellent public speaker can become a unifying presence and can bring about solidarity within their audience.

Preventing and Resolving Problems

Public speaking skills can help individuals to identify and resolve problems quickly and effectively. The mastery of idea synthesis and summation that a good public speaker possesses becomes useful in a whole range of troubleshooting tasks that require groups of people to come together and address problems.

Having good public speaking skills can also provide us with the tools necessary to prevent problems from arising in the first place. Our increased aptitudes for calling foul, when necessary allow us to take on more active roles as whistleblowers. When we do not have a fear of speaking out, we can be more well-poised to address problems as they arise rather than letting them go until they reach the breaking point.

Always approaching problems from a positive, productive standpoint, a good public speaker does not raise issues with things simply to point out flaws but to propose real, actionable solutions.

Providing a Sense of Direction

Developing good public speaking skills can help provide individuals with a clear sense of direction, enabling them to clearly articulate their goals and objectives. When we think in a focused and organized way about how to best organize and present our ideas, we are able to liberate ourselves from the shoulder-shrugging state of not knowing that sometimes can bog us all down.

Through our clear, targeted, and consistent messaging, we are able to create guiding trajectories which aid in keeping us on track in life. It is not about rigidity but about having a clear path defined. The ability to implement these ideas successfully helps us surmount walls of worry and allows us to move forward in life with a clear sense of direction.

Providing Clarity of Thoughts

Developing great public speaking skills enables individuals to better express their thoughts and ideas with clarity and precision, leading to better communication and understanding in all types of contexts. It allows us to hone our ideas and make them more effective and poignant. When we deliver these messages, it is our intentional, well-honed clarity of thought that allows us to deliver our messages in the thoughtful, well-crafted formats that they take.

In turn, these skills can affect our lives across more broad areas, giving us the ability to think more clearly in all types of situations, even under stressful ones. By applying the same skills that we learn to outwardly project the messages that are important to us, we can, in turn, direct those same things inwards, providing better quality and resolution to our internal thoughts and feelings.

To Sum Things Up

The benefits of public speaking skills are numerous, and they have a positive impact on both personal and professional life. With good public speaking skills, individuals can become better leaders, communicators, and problem-solvers, leading to a more fulfilling life across a broad spectrum of areas.

Chapter 3
Tips to Improve Your Public Speaking

As we emphasized before, public speaking is a skill that can be learned and honed with practice. In this chapter, we will discuss some easy-to-follow tips to help you enhance your communication skills and become a public speaking whiz.

The tips 18 that we will be covering in this section include:

- Do not fidget.
- Focus on brevity and clarity.
- Check your message.
- Do not be afraid of silence.
- Do not cross your arms.
- Bridge the gaps and maintain the flow.
- Avoid "ums" and "uhs."
- The audience is paramount.
- Maintain good posture.
- Think Positive!
- Make eye contact.
- Smile!
- Practice active listening.
- Be self-aware.
- Speak up!
- Think before you speak.
- Do not make assumptions.
- Be mindful of your body language.

Fidgeting

To avoid distracting your audience, try to minimize any unnecessary movements, such as tapping your foot, playing with your hair, or pacing back and forth. Standing still with a confident posture can help you project confidence and authority.

Brevity and Clarity

It is essential to cut to the chase while communicating, especially during public speaking. Being concise and specific in your message can help you hold your audience's attention and ensure that they understand it clearly. Make sure to cut out any redundant or repetitive content before presenting, and always make sure that your concepts are refined and your messages clear.

Checking Your Message

Before delivering your message, make sure to check it for accuracy. This is an essential step in the speech preparation process that will allow you to avoid any misunderstandings and miscommunication. Always double-check hard facts, statistics, suggestions, or allegations that are included in the content of your speech. Ensure that all data points and conjectures are true to the best of your knowledge and are backed up with research and hard data when necessary.

Silence

Silence is an essential tool in public speaking, and it can help you emphasize important points or give your audience a moment to absorb your message. Do not be afraid to pause and take a breath now and then to maintain control over the pace of your speech. You do not want to blurt everything out at once and rush through your speech. Make sure to maintain an even pace while speaking.

You can also use pauses for emphasis or to give your audience an opportunity to think about the ideas you pose or ask questions.

Making Sure Not to Cross Your Arms

Crossing your arms can signal defensiveness or a lack of openness to your audience. To appear confident and approachable, try to keep your arms relaxed and open. Some people have the tendency to do this without even thinking. If it helps, try to use hand gestures that will prevent you from crossing your arms. If you are seated during your speech, you can clasp your hands together in a gesture of confidence and self-assurance.

Bridging Topics and Maintaining Flow

If you need to change the topic or shift the conversation, try to find a connection between the new and old topics. Finding a bridge can help your audience follow your thought process and stay engaged. Make sure your transition between subject matter and conversation points is smooth and not jumpy. Try not to sound tangential while still maintaining your audience's interest. Jotting down notes that mark transition points between topics can help you accomplish this.

Avoiding "um's" and "uh's."

Using filler words such as "um" and "uh" can weaken your message and undermine your authority on the subject matter. Practice pausing or taking a breath instead of relying on filler words to bridge gaps. If your presentation includes an image deck or slideshow, you can fill any issues with witty banter. Saying something like, "Just bear with me for one second," is more reassuring to the audience than saying something like, "Um…, it is not loading." Take any technical failures in your presentation with grace and maintain composure. These things are bound to happen, and staying relaxed when they do occur will make you come across as confident and comfortable.

Giving Due Importance to Your Audience

Remember to focus on your audience's needs and interests. Tailor your message to their level of knowledge and use language they can understand. When appropriate, rely on your audience for feedback and participation during your speech, giving them cues that will encourage their active engagement. Do not bore them with unnecessary information. If the subject matter you are presenting is dense and technical, check in with them from time to time to make sure everything is clear or if they want you to repeat anything.

Maintaining Good Posture

Your posture can have a significant impact on how your audience perceives you. Maintain an open, upright posture to convey confidence and authority. Keep your shoulders back and your chin slightly raised. If you need to glance at your notes or computer screen occasionally, make sure to do so in a way that does not divert your attention from your audience. You do not want to come off like you are reading off a script. Keeping good posture and form throughout your speech will help you project your voice. Keeping your chest slightly puffed out, rather than slumping down with your stomach extended, will help you speak from your diaphragm. When you inhale, breathe in through your nose, making a conscious effort to fill your lungs rather than puffing out your stomach.

Maintaining a Positive Attitude

A positive attitude can be contagious, and it can help you build rapport and connection with your audience. Try to convey enthusiasm and energy while speaking. Coming off as genuine to your audience is important, so there is no need to go over the top with performative displays of energy and enthusiasm, but try to focus on projecting a positive mood and cultivating a good rapport with your audience. One of the most important parts of speech preparation is making sure you wake up on the right side of the bed. Get a good night's sleep, and practice healthy habits the day of that will allow you to show up fully. Make sure you are not hungry or tired during your speech. Try to eat something that will supercharge you before your speech, like fresh juice made with fruits and vegetables.

Making Eye Contact

Maintaining eye contact while speaking can help you connect with your audience and convey sincerity and confidence. You can connect with individual audience members this way and drive in points while keeping them engaged. Maintaining eye contact with a large group is impossible, but if you pick a few key audience members, you will have a much easier time conceptualizing how to approach this. The key here is making the connection, not necessarily locking your eyes with various members the entire time. So do not stress out about it, just give it a go, and you will see the wonders it can do for you.

Smiling

Smiling can help you appear more approachable and friendly, and it can help put your audience at ease. This is especially important when it comes to presenting in front of strangers. A neutral expression can make it seem like you are under stress or duress or can make your words seem overly serious, while a smile can make you appear at ease. Make sure your smile is coming from a genuine place. To this, you will have to bring authentic, live energy to the table, something you can do by making sure to practice all the healthy habits we previously mentioned the day of your specs and by being well-prepared.

Active Listening

Active listening involves fully engaging with your audience and responding appropriately to their feedback or questions. It can help you build rapport and connection with your audience. If your speech includes a Q&A section or has moments of back-and-forth interaction within it, use body language techniques like nodding your head to affirm the questions and thoughts of your audience. Use positive affirmations like "great question" or "I hadn't thought about it that way, but now that you mention it…" to let your audience know that you appreciate their thoughtful feedback."

Self-Awareness

Being aware of your strengths and weaknesses can help you improve your public speaking skills. Identify areas that need improvement and work on developing them. Being self-aware is about being comfortable in your skin; to do that, you must first confront your fears and weaknesses head-on. For some, having an innate sense of self-awareness, but for others, it requires a more conscious, active effort on their own part. I have certainly had my own struggles in this area, and I have managed to maintain good lessons of self-awareness through physical alignment practices and consciousness exercises through yoga and meditation. Unfortunately, there is not one specific pre-prescribed way of going about this; instead, everyone being the unique individuals we are, must look inwards and find their own paths toward self-awareness.

Speaking Up

Speaking up can help you convey your message clearly and confidently. You do not want to be shouting, but you want to make sure your voice projects. It is not about volume but about the amplitude with which you project. Speak from your diaphragm, not from your throat and nasal cavity. Some of us are naturally timider and more soft-spoken, and this area can be especially difficult for us to develop. Make sure you do not trail off at the end of your sentences. While you are speaking, take a look at the furthest people in the room; just reading their facial expressions will tell you a lot about whether they can hear you or not. If they have a puzzled expression, it may be that they cannot hear you. Do not be afraid to ask your audience if they can hear you well. If they cannot hear you well, remember: Amplitude, not volume, and speak from your diaphragm.

Thinking Before You Speak

As mentioned previously, you do not want to come off like you are reading from a script. Peppering your speeches with some off-the-cuff remarks can be a great way to make your speech memorable. One of the ways to aid in this is to improvise and include some unrehearsed, candid moments in your speech. When you do incorporate these moments, make sure to think before you say them.

Consider any unrehearsed or slightly tangential messages you want to convey before simply blurting them out. You want to appear natural but also to avoid venturing too far off your topic and diverting attention from your core message. Thinking before you speak in real-time while under the pressure of a public speaking engagement is a very difficult thing to accomplish. But once you are able to do it successfully, you will find that the results are well worth the extra effort.

Avoiding Making Assumptions

Assumptions can lead to misunderstandings and miscommunication. Try to clarify any ambiguities or uncertainties in your speech material before delivering your message. You are also going to want to avoid making too many assumptions about your audience. Ask them questions about their experience or preferences rather than generalizing. Try to avoid assessing situations in terms that might neglect or make some audience members uncomfortable. Do not be afraid of being honest about the complexities of problems or situations you are presenting; rather, focus on streamlining them in a way that will open up new dialogues between yourself and your audience.

Being Mindful of Your Body Language

Your body language can convey just as much meaning as your words. Practice using open and confident body language to reinforce your message. You do not want to appear too uptight or rigid. What you do want is for your body movements and gestures to match the pace and rhythms of your speech. Practice in front of a trusted friend to make sure that your body language comes off as natural. Though it may sound counterintuitive, you need to practice this to make sure it does not come off as seeming rehearsed. Think about the flows of your talking points and embody them.

To Sum Things Up

These tips can help anyone improve their public speaking skills and become a more confident communicator. Remember that effective communication is not just about speaking but also about active listening, self-awareness, and nonverbal communication. It takes practice and patience to become a skilled speaker, but with these tips in mind, you can become a more engaging and effective communicator in any setting. Keep practicing, and do not be afraid to step outside your comfort zone. With time and effort, you can become a more confident and effective public speaker.

Book 4:
Speak Up and Slay

Overcoming Public Speaking Anxiety
and Delivering Killer Presentations

Kirsten Rae Evans

TABLE OF CONTENTS

Introduction 133

Chapter 1: Identifying Social Anxiety 135
    Identify Social Anxiety 135
    Emotional and Behavioral Symptoms 135
    Physical Symptoms 138
    The Causes of Social Anxiety 140
    Complications That Can Arise From Social Anxiety 142

Chapter 2: Overcoming Public Speaking Anxiety 145

Chapter 3: Cure for Public Speaking Anxiety 153
    Managing Your Anxiety 154
    Living a Healthy Lifestyle 155
    Keeping Tabs on Your Habits 156
    Tips That Can Help You Overcome
    Public Speaking Anxiety 157
    How to Embrace Change and Transformation 159

Introduction

In this book, we will first delve into the reasons behind public speaking anxiety and then offer you a toolkit to help overcome them. By providing you with practical strategies that can help you conquer your fear, boost your confidence, and captivate any audience, you will have access to a roadmap to start improving your public speaking skills.

Whether you are presenting in a professional setting, delivering a persuasive speech, or engaging in a public debate, the ability to communicate confidently and effectively is paramount. If you take the lessons covered in this book seriously, soon enough, your speeches will slay, and you will be saying to yourself: "Where would I be today if I never learned to speak up?"

Chapter 1
Identifying Social Anxiety

Social anxiety is a mental health disorder that affects a person's ability to communicate effectively in social situations. This chapter focuses on identifying the various symptoms, causes, and complications of social anxiety.

Identify Social Anxiety

Social anxiety is best understood as an unmitigated or persistent fear of social situations. This means that it is not something that defines us but something that can be overcome with the right resources. It can manifest in various emotional and physical symptoms, as well as impact a person's overall well-being. In this section, we will explore the emotional and physical symptoms associated with social anxiety.

Emotional and Behavioral Symptoms

Social anxiety can lead to various emotional and behavioral symptoms. Some of the common symptoms can leave people paralyzed by fear and unable to move forward in life. It is something we all face to a certain degree, but for some more than others, it represents a difficulty that must be successfully overcome *before* great public speaking skills can be successfully developed.

The emotional and behavioral symptoms of social anxiety that we will be covering in this section include

- Over-analyzing your performance
- Anxiety over specific activities or events
- Anxiety over social gatherings
- Anxiety over being the center of attention
- Avoidant behavior and fear of talking to strangers
- Difficulty making eye contact
- Difficulty starting conversations
- Difficulty with eating in front of others
- Discomfort in crowds
- Fixation on negative experiences or interactions at social events
- Fear of displaying physical symptoms of anxiety while talking to strangers
- Fear of judgment
- Fear of using public restrooms
- Fear of public embarrassment

Being Over-Analytical of Your Performance

This common pitfall can lead to excessive self-criticism, which in turn can worsen social anxiety.

Being Anxious About Specific Activities or Events

This can include social situations such as meetings or parties, as well as public speaking events or job interviews.

Being Anxious Over Social Gatherings

People with social anxiety may feel uncomfortable in social gatherings and may avoid them altogether.

Having Anxiety Over Being the Center of Attention

This can include situations where you may have to speak or perform in front of others.

Displaying Avoidant Behavior Around Strangers

This can include avoiding social interactions in public places such as elevators or waiting rooms.

Having Difficulty Making Eye Contact

People with social anxiety may struggle to maintain eye contact during conversations.

Having Difficulty With Starting Conversations

Initiating a conversation can be a challenging task for people with social anxiety.

Being Anxious When Eating in Front of Others

This can include eating in public places such as restaurants, break rooms, or cafeterias.

Being Anxious in Large Crowds

People with social anxiety may feel overwhelmed in crowded places.

Fixating on Negative Social Interactions

This can lead to a vicious cycle of negative thinking and avoidance behaviors.

Being Afraid of Appearing Anxious Around Others

People with social anxiety may fear blushing, sweating, or shaking during social interactions.

Being Afraid of Being Judged by Others

This can include situations where you may be evaluated, such as job interviews or public speaking events.

Being Afraid of Using Public Restrooms

This can be a challenging task for people with social anxiety.

Being Afraid of Public Embarrassing Yourself in Public

This can lead to avoidance behaviors and social isolation.

Physical Symptoms

Social anxiety can also lead to various physical symptoms, such as an upset stomach, blushing, and sweating. It is important to recognize the symptoms to get an idea of whether you have ever been afflicted with and held back by social anxiety.

The physical symptoms of social anxiety that we will be covering in this section include

- blushing
- dizziness
- blank-mindedness
- muscle tension and spasms
- nausea

- rapid heartbeat
- sweating
- trembling and shaking
- respiratory difficulties

Blushing

People with social anxiety may experience sudden redness in their faces during social interactions.

Dizziness

This can include lightheadedness or vertigo.

Blank-Mindedness

The feeling that your mind has gone blank. People with social anxiety may experience difficulty thinking or speaking during social interactions.

Muscle Tension

This can include tightness in the chest, neck, or shoulders.

Nausea

People with social anxiety may experience stomach discomfort or nausea during social interactions.

Rapid Heartbeat

This can include a rapid or irregular heartbeat.

Sweating

People with social anxiety may experience excessive sweating, especially in the hands or underarms.

Trembling and Shaking

This can include shaking or quivering of the hands, legs, or voice.

Respiratory Difficulties

Trouble catching your breath. This can include shortness of breath or hyperventilation.

The Causes of Social Anxiety

Social anxiety can have various causes, some genetic and others learned or culturally ingrained.

The causes of social anxiety that we will be covering in this section include

- Brain structure
- Family history and genetics
- Physical difference/appearance
- Negative experiences and trauma
- New social demands or work responsibilities
- Surrounding environment
- Temperament/personality traits

Brain Structure

Social anxiety can be related to specific brain structures and neurotransmitters, such as the amygdala and serotonin (Martin et al., 2009).

Family History and Genetics

Social anxiety can run in families, indicating that a genetic predisposition may exist. Furthermore, social conditioning, as well as family structure and dynamics, can also contribute to our likelihood of developing social anxiety.

Physical Difference / Appearance

People with physical abnormalities or disabilities may be more prone to social anxiety, as they often catch glares and face discrimination from others. Though it is an unfortunate reality, even in today's society which values openness and diversity—disabled people are often left behind.

Negative Experiences and Trauma

Traumatic experiences such as bullying or public humiliation can contribute to social anxiety in many ways. For example, if someone is ridiculed or made fun of during a public speaking event, they may develop a fear of public speaking or socializing in general. Similarly, being bullied or harassed can lead to feelings of shame and inadequacy, which can then manifest as social anxiety.

New Social or Work-Related Demands

New social or work demands can also trigger social anxiety. For instance, starting a new job or joining a new social group can be challenging for someone who struggles with social anxiety. The pressure to perform well and fit in can be overwhelming and lead to increased anxiety.

Our Surrounding Environment

The surrounding environment can also contribute to social anxiety. People who live in areas with high levels of crime or violence may feel unsafe and avoid social situations altogether. Additionally, people who grow up in households with overprotective or critical parents may have difficulty developing social skills and confidence.

Temperament and Personality Traits

Temperament and our personality conditioning can also play a role in the development of social anxiety. Some people are naturally more shy or introverted, which can make social situations more challenging for them. However, it is important to note that social anxiety is not simply a personality trait and can be overcome with the right treatment and support.

Complications That Can Arise From Social Anxiety

There are several complications that can arise from social anxiety, making things even more difficult for those afflicted.

The complications that can arise from social anxiety that we will be covering in this section include

- Difficulty developing and maintaining relationships
- Hypersensitivity to criticism
- Isolation
- Low self-esteem
- Negative self-talk
- Poor social skills
- Substance abuse
- Suicide or suicide attempts
- Difficulty being assertive

Having Difficulty Developing and Maintaining Relationships

People with social anxiety may have difficulty making friends or maintaining romantic relationships due to their fear of social situations. They may have a fear of starting new relationships based on fears that, like previous ones, they will inevitably fail.

Being Hypersensitive to Criticism

People with social anxiety may be overly sensitive to criticism or negative feedback, further eroding their self-esteem and confidence. They may lash out in response to feeling threatened or humiliated by seemingly benign comments.

Feeling Isolated

Avoiding social situations can lead to isolation, which can exacerbate feelings of loneliness and depression. People with social anxiety can end up feeling trapped this way.

Engaging in Negative Self-Talk

People with social anxiety may engage in negative self-talk, such as telling themselves they are not good enough or will embarrass themselves in social situations.

Having Low Self-Esteem

Constant negative self-talk and self-doubt can lead to low self-esteem, which can further contribute to social anxiety. These negative self-criticisms can make people with social anxiety feel that they are not worthy.

Having Poor Social Skills

Avoiding social situations can prevent people with social anxiety from developing and practicing social skills, which can lead to difficulty communicating with others and building relationships.

Engaging in Substance Abuse

Some people with social anxiety may turn to drugs or alcohol as a way to cope with their anxiety, which can lead to substance abuse and addiction.

Thinking About Suicide or Making Suicide Attempts

In severe cases, social anxiety can lead to suicidal thoughts or attempts.

Having Trouble With Asserting Oneself

People with social anxiety may have difficulty being assertive or standing up for themselves in social or professional situations.

To Sum Things Up

Social anxiety disorder can significantly impact an individual's quality of life, making it difficult to perform day-to-day activities and form meaningful relationships. It is crucial to identify the symptoms of social anxiety and take steps to address the underlying causes to overcome the disorder. Seeking professional help, practicing relaxation techniques, and gradually exposing oneself to anxiety-provoking situations can help alleviate the symptoms of social anxiety and improve one's overall well-being. By understanding the causes and effects of social anxiety disorder, individuals can take the necessary steps to overcome this debilitating condition and lead a more fulfilling life.

Chapter 2

Overcoming Public Speaking Anxiety

Public speaking anxiety can be debilitating, but overcoming it can bring about numerous benefits. This chapter will discuss the various benefits of overcoming public speaking anxiety and how they can help you achieve your personal and professional goals.

The benefits of overcoming public speaking anxiety that we will be covering in this section include the following:

- It will improve your listening skills.
- It will let you advocate for yourself and others.
- It will boost your confidence.
- It will boost your leadership skills.
- It will help increase your social connections.

Becoming a Better Listener

Overcoming public speaking anxiety can help you become a better listener by allowing you to focus more on what others are saying. By overcoming your fear, you can be present in the moment and listen to the messages that others are conveying.

Becoming a Powerful Advocate

Effective public speaking can help you become a powerful advocate for your ideas, values, and causes. By overcoming your fear, you can deliver persuasive speeches and presentations that can inspire others to act.

Boosting Your Confidence

Overcoming public speaking anxiety can boost your confidence and self-esteem. Once you conquer your fear, you will feel more confident in your abilities and be better equipped to handle challenging situations.

Strengthening Your Leadership Skills

Public speaking is a crucial skill for leaders. By overcoming public speaking anxiety, you can develop your leadership skills and become a more effective communicator.

Building Your Social Connections

Public speaking can help you build social connections and expand your network. By overcoming your fear, you can network with like-minded individuals and make valuable connections that can benefit your personal and professional life.

Advancing Your Career

Effective public speaking can help you advance in your career. By overcoming public speaking anxiety, you can deliver engaging presentations and speeches that can impress your colleagues and superiors.

Developing Your Nonverbal Communication Skills

Public speaking involves not just verbal communication but also nonverbal communication. By overcoming public speaking anxiety, you can develop your body language skills and convey confidence and authority.

Enriching Your Vocabulary

Public speaking can help you develop a good vocabulary and improve your language skills. By overcoming your fear, you can practice and improve your speech and language, making you a better communicator.

Eliminating the Fear of Public Speaking

Overcoming public speaking anxiety eliminates the fear associated with public speaking. By conquering this fear, you can enjoy public speaking and the opportunities it brings.

Enhancing Your Critical Thinking Skills

Public speaking requires critical thinking and analysis. By overcoming public speaking anxiety, you can enhance your critical thinking skills and become a better problem solver.

Enhancing Your Public Speaking Capabilities

Though it may sound obvious or redundant, overcoming public speaking anxiety can help you enhance your public speaking skills. You can become a more effective communicator and deliver powerful presentations by practicing and refining your skills.

Enhancing Your Ability to Exercise Deductive Reasoning

Public speaking requires deductive reasoning, analysis, and problem-solving. By overcoming your fear, you can improve your ability to exercise deductive reasoning and think critically.

Helping Yourself Expand Your Network of Social and Business Contacts

Effective public speaking can help you expand your network and build new relationships. By overcoming public speaking anxiety, you can network with like-minded individuals and create new opportunities for growth.

Helping Yourself Learn the Skills Necessary to Drive Change

Effective public speaking can help you drive change and create a positive impact. By overcoming your fear, you can inspire and motivate others to act.

Improving Your Communication Skills

Public speaking is a powerful tool for improving communication skills. By overcoming public speaking anxiety, you can improve your ability to communicate clearly and effectively.

Increasing Your Professional Success

Effective public speaking can increase your professional success and help you achieve your career goals. By overcoming public speaking anxiety, you can deliver powerful presentations and speeches that can impress your colleagues and superiors.

Inspiring Others

Overcoming public speaking anxiety can help you inspire others and share your ideas and visions effectively. By delivering a powerful message and engaging with your audience, you can motivate and influence others to act toward a common goal. For example, many famous leaders are known for their exceptional public speaking skills, which helped them inspire millions of people and bring about significant changes.

Learning Performance Skills

Public speaking can be thought of as a performance. By overcoming your fear of public speaking, you will learn performance skills that can be applied to other areas of your life, such as acting or singing.

Learning the Art of Persuasion

Public speaking is a valuable tool for learning the art of persuasion. When you speak in public, you have the opportunity to persuade your audience to believe in your ideas, to take a certain action, or to support a particular cause. Effective persuasion requires using the right language, tone, and body language and being able to anticipate and address potential objections or concerns. By overcoming public speaking anxiety and gaining the requisite skills, you can learn to be a more persuasive communicator and make a more significant impact on your audience.

Learning to Be More Observant

Public speaking can also help you develop your observational skills. When you speak in public, you need to be aware of your audience's reactions, body language, and other non-verbal cues. Being able to read and respond to your audience effectively can help you tailor your message and make a stronger connection with them. In addition, the process of preparing for a speech can help you become more observant in general, as you may need to conduct research, gather information, and analyze data to develop your message.

Overcoming Your Fears

Overcoming public speaking anxiety can be a significant personal accomplishment. By facing your fears and working to improve your public speaking skills, you can gain a sense of empowerment and confidence that can extend to other areas of your life. This can help you feel more in control of your thoughts and emotions and more prepared to face new challenges in the future.

Increasing Your Personal Satisfaction

Being able to deliver a powerful and effective speech can be a rewarding and fulfilling experience. It can give you a sense of personal satisfaction and achievement and help you feel more confident and self-assured. Additionally, knowing that you have the skills to speak confidently in public can help you feel more prepared and in control in a variety of situations.

Making Your Research Skills More Effective and Impactful

Preparing for a speech requires conducting research, gathering information, and analyzing data to develop a compelling message. By honing your research skills, you can become more effective and impactful in all areas of your life, not just in public speaking. You can learn to identify reliable sources, analyze data effectively, and present information in a clear and compelling way. This can help you make better decisions, solve problems more effectively, and communicate more effectively in a variety of settings.

To Sum Things Up

Overall, overcoming public speaking anxiety can offer a wide range of benefits, both personally and professionally. By developing your public speaking skills, you can become a more effective communicator, build stronger relationships, inspire others, and make a more significant impact on the world around you.

CHAPTER 3

CURE FOR PUBLIC SPEAKING ANXIETY

Overcoming public speaking, anxiety can be achieved by challenging negative thoughts and converting them into positive ones, along with adopting various other effective strategies.

The ways to overcome public speaking anxiety that we will be covering in this section include

- Being more mindful of your anxiety and its triggers
- Not relying on substances like alcohol
- Being mindful of avoidance behavior
- Engaging in public speaking role-playing exercises
- Doing kind things for others
- Practicing breathing exercises and meditation
- Getting more comfortable with small talk
- Giving good handshakes
- Challenging yourself by exposure to anxiety-inducing situations
- Practicing gratitude
- Advocating for yourself
- Eating a healthy diet
- Getting alone time
- Getting sufficient amounts of exercise

- Getting sufficient amounts of sleep
- Making sure to laugh
- Keeping a journal
- Living a healthy lifestyle
- Making one change at a time
- Putting social skills into practice
- Practicing yoga
- Reading books
- Rewarding yourself
- Setting smart goals
- Spending time in nature
- Stopping the blame game and constant complaining
- Stopping putting things off
- Stopping thinking that nothing will work out
- Stopping trying to be perfect
- Stopping waiting to be rescued
- Taking a vacation
- Working with your strengths

Managing Your Anxiety

One of the best ways to manage anxiety is to identify your triggers and negative thoughts.

How to Examine the Situations That Trigger Your Anxiety

1. Identify the situations that trigger your anxiety.
2. Write down your experiences, feelings, and thoughts to become more aware of them.
3. Challenge negative thoughts.

How to Identify the Negative Thoughts That Feed Your Anxiety

1. Challenge these thoughts with more realistic and positive ones.
2. Practice positive affirmations to boost your confidence.

Living a Healthy Lifestyle

Making healthy lifestyle choices, such as avoiding smoking and excessive alcohol consumption, can help improve your overall health and reduce anxiety.

- Eat a healthy balanced diet: Eating a balanced and healthy diet can help improve your overall health and mood. This can help you better manage anxiety and stress.
- Try relaxation techniques: Breathing exercises, meditation, and progressive muscle relaxation can help you relax and reduce anxiety. Practicing relaxation techniques regularly can help build your resilience to stress.
- Do not rely on alcohol or other substances: Alcohol and other substances may initially make you feel relaxed, but they can also impair your judgment and coordination and increase your anxiety.
- Practice yoga or martial arts: Yoga is a great way to reduce stress and anxiety, which can help you feel calm and centered before a public speaking engagement. Certain yoga poses, such as the tree pose, can also help improve your posture and confidence. You can also try relaxing martial arts practices like tai chi or qigong.
- Get exercise: Regular exercise can help improve your mood and reduce anxiety. Aim for at least 30 minutes of moderate exercise per day.
- Make sure you get adequate sleep: Getting enough sleep is essential for managing stress and anxiety. Aim for 7-9 hours of sleep per night.

- Laugh more often: Laughter can help reduce stress and anxiety. Find ways to incorporate humor into your life, such as watching a funny movie or spending time with friends who make you laugh.

Keeping Tabs on Your Habits

Watch Out for the More Subtle Forms of Avoidance Behavior

- Remember that avoiding situations that cause anxiety can actually make the problem worse.
- Challenge yourself to confront your fears and gradually work your way up to speaking in public.

Stop Complaining and Blaming

Focusing on negative thoughts and blaming others for your anxiety will only make the problem worse. Instead, try to adopt a more positive mindset and take responsibility for your thoughts and actions.

Stop Putting Things Off

Procrastination can be a major contributor to public speaking anxiety. By tackling tasks and responsibilities in a timely manner, you can reduce stress and anxiety and feel more prepared for your speaking engagements.

Stop Thinking Nothing Will Work Out for You

It is easy to fall into the trap of thinking that nothing will work when it comes to overcoming public speaking anxiety. However, with the right mindset and strategies, anyone can improve their public speaking skills and overcome their anxiety.

Stop Trying to Be Perfect

Perfectionism can be a major obstacle to public speaking success. Instead of striving for perfection, focus on doing your best and learning from your mistakes.

Stop Waiting to Be Rescued

No one else can overcome your public speaking anxiety for you. It is important to take responsibility for your growth and development and take proactive steps toward overcoming your anxiety.

Tips That Can Help You Overcome Public Speaking Anxiety

Role Play Public Speaking Scenarios With Trusted People

- Practicing speaking in front of others can help reduce anxiety.
- Consider role-playing with people you trust, such as a close friend or family member.

Practice Acts of Kindness

- Doing something kind for someone else can help reduce anxiety.
- Volunteer for a cause you believe in or do something nice for a friend or family member.

Start Greeting Your Neighbors

- Practice small talk with people you encounter on a regular basis, such as neighbors.
- This can help you become more comfortable with social situations.

Strike Up a Conversation

- Initiate conversations with people you do not know well, such as coworkers or classmates.
- This can help you become more comfortable with initiating and engaging in conversations.

Practice Giving Great Handshakes

- A confident and firm handshake can help convey confidence and make a good impression.
- Practice giving a good handshake to help boost your confidence.

Take Small Steps, and be Kind to Yourself

- Gradually expose yourself to situations that trigger anxiety, starting with less challenging situations and working your way up.
- This can help you build your confidence and resilience.

Appreciate What You Have

- Practice gratitude by focusing on the things you are thankful for in your life.
- This can help shift your focus away from negative thoughts and improve your overall mood.

Become Your Best Advocate

- Advocate for yourself by speaking up for your needs and values.
- This can help you build confidence and assertiveness.

Embrace Alone Time

- Spending time alone can help you relax and recharge.
- This can also help you become more comfortable with being alone and reduce social anxiety.

Journal

- Journaling can help you process your thoughts and feelings and gain perspective.
- Write down your thoughts and experiences related to public speaking anxiety to help identify patterns and develop coping strategies.

How to Embrace Change and Transformation

Make One Change at a Time

When trying to overcome public speaking anxiety, it is important to take small steps and make one change at a time. This will help you avoid getting overwhelmed and will allow you to build your confidence gradually. For example, start by practicing your speech in front of a small group of friends or family members before giving a presentation to a larger audience.

Put Your Social Skills to Good Use

Public speaking involves more than just speaking; it also involves social skills such as active listening, empathy, and rapport building. By practicing these skills in everyday situations, you can improve your ability to connect with your audience and build trust.

Read a Book

Reading books can help moderate your internal levels of anxiety and can provide you with valuable insights and strategies for how to best approach life.

Reward Yourself

When you achieve a milestone in your public speaking journey, it is important to reward yourself. This will help reinforce positive behaviors and encourage you to continue working towards your goals. Rewards can be as simple as treating yourself to your favorite dessert or taking a day off to do something you enjoy.

Set SMART Goals for Yourself

Setting goals that are Specific, Measurable, Attainable, Realistic, and Time-bound (SMART) can help you stay focused and motivated. For example, you might set a goal to give a speech in front of a small audience within the next month or attend a public speaking workshop within the next six months.

Spend Time in Nature

Spending time in nature can help reduce stress and anxiety, which can have a positive impact on your public speaking performance. Whether it is taking a walk in the park or going on a hike, spending time in nature can help clear your mind and improve your mood.

Take a Vacation

Taking a break and getting away from the stresses of everyday life can help you recharge and feel more relaxed and refreshed before your next public speaking engagement.

Work With Your Innate Strengths

Everyone has their unique strengths and weaknesses when it comes to public speaking. By focusing on your strengths and leveraging them to your advantage, you can feel more confident and effective in your speaking engagements.

Book 5: The Persuasive Speaker

Mastering the Art of Influence and Winning Audiences Over

Kirsten Rae Evans

Table of Contents

Introduction 167

Chapter 1: Influence Your Audience 169
    Principles of Persuasion 171

Chapter 2: The Benefits of Influencing Skills 175

Chapter 3: Tips to Persuade Your Audience 179
    Design an Effective Introduction 180
    Tailor Content to your Listeners' Interest 182
    Guide your Listeners 184
    Design an Effective Conclusion 184

INTRODUCTION

In today's world, public speaking has become an essential skill for anyone who wants to succeed in their personal and professional life. Whether you are a CEO, a politician, a salesperson, or a student, the ability to communicate your ideas effectively and persuade others to act is critical. The power of persuasion lies in the hands of those who can connect with their audience and influence them in a meaningful way.

In this book, you will learn how to craft a compelling message, structure your presentation for maximum impact, use language and visuals effectively, and deliver your speech with confidence and charisma. You will also learn how to connect with your audience on an emotional level, build rapport, and persuade them to act.

Chapter 1
Influence Your Audience

In today's world, being able to influence and persuade others is a vital skill, especially for public speakers. Now, we will explore the different types of influence and principles of persuasion that can help you win over your audience.

The types of influence that we will be covering in this section include

- Asserting
- Bridging
- Inspiring
- Negotiating
- Rationalizing

Asserting Influence

Asserting influence is about being confident and firm in persuading your audience. This can be accomplished by using strong, clear language and body language to emphasize your points. For example, imagine you are a salesperson using assertive language to persuade a potential customer to purchase their product.

Bridging Influence

Bridging influence is about building connections with your audience to establish a sense of trust and understanding. This can be accomplished by finding common ground and highlighting shared experiences or interests. For example, imagine you are a politician using personal anecdotes to connect with voters and gain their trust.

Inspiring Influence

Inspiring influence is about motivating and inspiring your audience to act or change their perspectives. This can be accomplished by sharing inspiring stories, quotes, or examples that appeal to your audience's emotions. For example, imagine that you are a motivational speaker using personal stories and examples to inspire your audience to pursue their goals.

Negotiating Influence

Negotiating influence is about finding a compromise that satisfies both you and your audience. This can be accomplished by identifying common goals and working together to find a mutually beneficial solution. For example, imagine that you are a business executive negotiating with employees to find a solution that benefits both the company and its workers.

Rationalizing Influence

Rationalizing influence is about presenting logical arguments to persuade your audience. This can be accomplished using data, statistics, and logical reasoning to support your points. For example, imagine that you are a scientist using empirical evidence to persuade your audience of your research findings.

Principles of Persuasion

The principles of persuasion that we will be covering in this section include

- Authority
- Consistency
- Reciprocity
- Scarcity
- Social proof
- Sympathy

Authority

Authority is about establishing credibility and expertise in your field to gain your audience's trust. This can be accomplished by citing your credentials, experience, or qualifications. For example, imagine you are a doctor using their medical degree and experience to persuade their patients to follow a specific treatment plan.

Consistency

Consistency is about emphasizing the importance of keeping one's promises and being consistent in one's actions and beliefs.

This can be accomplished by highlighting past actions or decisions that demonstrate consistency. For example, imagine you are a politician emphasizing their consistent voting record on a particular issue.

Reciprocity

Reciprocity is about giving before receiving to create a sense of obligation and gratitude in your audience. This can be accomplished by offering something of value before asking for something in return. For example, imagine that you run a charity organization and decide to offer a small gift to potential donors before asking for a donation.

Scarcity

Scarcity is about creating a sense of urgency or exclusivity to persuade your audience to act or decide. This can be accomplished by highlighting limited availability, time-sensitive offers, or unique opportunities. For example, imagine you are a store owner, and you decide to use limited-time sales or exclusive products to persuade customers to make a purchase.

Social Proof

Social proof is about using the actions and beliefs of others to persuade your audience to follow suit. This can be accomplished by citing testimonials, reviews, or social media presence to demonstrate popularity and support. For example, imagine you run a company and decide to use customer reviews and testimonials to persuade potential customers to try your product.

Sympathy

Sympathy is about appealing to your audience's emotions and empathy to persuade them to act or decide. This can be accomplished using personal stories or examples that evoke sympathy or empathy. For example, imagine that you volunteer for a charity organization, and you decide to use stories of individuals in need to persuade donors to donate.

To Sum Things Up

Mastering the art of influence and persuasion is a powerful tool for any public speaker. By understanding the different types of influence and the principles of persuasion, you can create a compelling message that resonates with your audience and inspires them to act. Remember to always be authentic and genuine in your approach and use your powers of influence for good. By doing so, you will not only become a more effective speaker but also a positive force for change in the world.

Chapter 2
The Benefits of Influencing Skills

Improving your influencing skills is not just a valuable skill for public speakers, but it can also benefit your personal and professional life. We'll look into the various benefits of improving your influencing skills.

The benefits of improving your influencing skills that we will be covering in this section include

- Career advancement
- Sparks change in your audience
- Allows you to exercise your deductive reasoning and critical thinking skills
- Expands your network
- Expands your vocabulary
- Helps build confidence
- Helps develop leadership skills
- Helps your verbal communication
- Improves your research skills
- Persuades and informs others
- Allows you to implement your performance skills
- Helps you become a better listener
- Improves your influencing skills

Advancing Your Career

Influencing skills can help you advance in your career by allowing you to negotiate better salaries, secure promotions, and build a stronger professional network. It can make you well-known not just within your company but throughout your entire industry.

Advocating for Things That Matter to You

By improving your influencing skills, you can effectively advocate for topics you care about, whether in your personal or professional life. This, in turn, can lead to an increase in personal life satisfaction.

Sparking Change in Your Audience

Being able to influence and persuade your audience can lead to positive changes in their behavior or actions. Your words have the power to inspire others!

Exercising Your Deductive Reasoning and Critical Thinking Skills

Improving your influencing skills requires careful analysis and evaluation of information to present a convincing argument, which in turn exercises your deductive reasoning skills. Improving your influencing skills requires careful analysis and evaluation of information, which in turn can help strengthen your critical thinking skills.

Expanding Your Network

As you improve your influencing skills, you will likely meet more people and expand your network, which can open up new opportunities for you. Being influential can open up a whole new world of business opportunities and personal friendships for you to rely on.

Expanding Your Vocabulary

The more you practice influencing and persuading, the more you will develop your vocabulary and communication skills, which can benefit you in all areas of your life. You will learn how to incorporate vocabulary that is tailor-made for your audience, driving your core messages home.

Building Confidence

The ability to influence others can help build your confidence, both in your personal and professional life. This reinforcement of your confidence and internal drive can, in turn, allow you to stay motivated, an important part of maintaining influence.

Developing Leadership Skills

Improving your influencing skills can help develop your leadership skills, allowing you to motivate and inspire others. This can lead to new roles and responsibilities, accolades, and appreciation for your efforts.

Improving Your Verbal Communication Skills

The process of influencing others requires strong oral communication skills, and improving these skills can benefit you in all areas of your life. You will have an easier time navigating all kinds of complex situations.

Improving Your Research Skills

Influencing and persuading others requires careful research and analysis of information, which in turn can help improve your research skills. Your ability to effectively synthesize and convey information will be sharpened, making your public speaking even more influential.

Persuading and Informing Others

Influencing and persuading others is a valuable skill that can be used to both inform and persuade others. Remember—you are persuading your audience not to manipulate them but rather to open them up to your ideas and hopefully win them over. This is a privilege of possessing high influencing skills, not a granted right.

Applying Your Performance Skills

Improving your influencing skills can also help you develop your performance skills, allowing you to become a more effective interpreter of the ideas you want to show others. Remember—performance does not mean "acting,"; it means showing in an effective way.

Becoming a Better Listener

The process of influencing others requires active listening and understanding of your audience, which can help you become a better listener in all areas of your life. Remember—this can help you improve your business relationships, as well as your personal ones.

To Sum Things Up

Improving your influencing skills can benefit you in many ways, both personally and professionally. By understanding the various benefits, you can work towards improving your skills and becoming a more effective communicator and leader.

Chapter 3
Tips to Persuade Your Audience

The ability to persuade and influence is an essential skill for any public speaker. Whether it is to get your audience to act, change their minds or beliefs, or simply inform them, persuasive communication is key. In this chapter, we will discuss several tips to help you become a more persuasive speaker and win over your audience.

The tips for persuading your audience that we will be covering in this section include:

- Design an effective introduction.
- Ask a provocative question.
- Describe a scene or a character.
- Explain your interest in the topic.
- Offer a humorous observation or anecdote.
- Point out something important.
- Relate to a recent event.
- Share a personal experience.
- Show a compelling visual image.
- State a fact that is troubling, amusing, or remarkable.
- Tell a story.
- Tell the listeners what the topic has to do with them.

Design an Effective Introduction

The beginning of your speech is crucial for setting the tone and capturing your audience's attention. The tips for designing an effective introduction that we will be covering in this section include:

- Ask a provocative question.
- Continue with previous themes and remarks.
- Paint a picture for your audience.
- Explain your interest in the topic.
- Offer a humorous observation or anecdote.
- Point out something important about your topic.
- Relate your topic to a recent event.
- Share a personal experience of yours.
- Show a compelling visual image or graphic.
- State a fact that is troubling, amusing, or remarkable.
- Tell a story.
- Tell the listeners what the topic has to do with them.

Ask a Provocative Question

Ask your audience a question that will pique their curiosity and make them interested in your topic. This can be used as a lead-in to dissect a topic in more detail.

Continue with the Previous Speaker's Remarks or Theme

If you are speaking at an event where there were other speakers before you, reference their topic or speech to create a connection with your audience. You can also express your gratitude for being in the presence of the previous speakers and your audience.

Paint a Picture for Your Audience

Describe a scene or an archetypal character. Use your words to draw your audience in and help them visualize what you are talking about. Use a rich, descriptive vocabulary to emphasize your points.

Explain Your Interest in the Topic

Share a personal anecdote about why the topic is important to you. You can tell the audience how you first got interested in the subject matter and why you ended up where you are today.

Offer a Humorous Observation or Anecdote

Humor can help break the ice and make your audience more receptive to your message. Do not laugh too hard at your joke; let the audience do it for you.

Point out Something Important

Highlight a crucial fact or statistic that relates to your topic. Talk about the impact that it has, emphasizing its importance and relevance.

Relate to a Recent Event

Connect your topic to a recent news story or event that your audience will likely be familiar with. Relate your discourse to memes or cultural trends when appropriate.

Share a Personal Experience of Yours

Share a story from your life that relates to your topic. Try to humanize your understanding of the information being covered by revealing any previous deficits of knowledge in the area.

Show a Compelling Visual Image

Use a striking image or graphic related to your topic to capture your audience's attention. You can use humorous images when appropriate.

State a Fact that is Troubling, Amusing, or Remarkable

Share a fact or statistic that is surprising, amusing, or thought-provoking to make your audience sit up and take notice. Grab their attention with surprising data or findings.

Tell a Story

Storytelling is an effective way to engage your audience and make your message more memorable. Consider relaying personal anecdotes when appropriate or recounting stories about other people you know.

Tell the Listeners What the Topic Has to Do With Them

Explain why your topic matters to your audience and how it affects them. Explain in relatable terms how your ideas can have a positive impact or spark change.

Tailor Content to your Listeners' Interest

To persuade your audience, you need to tailor your message to their level of knowledge, experience, and interest. Think about it like you are customizing your speech to suit their needs, not like you are trying to wrap them around your idea.

The tips to gear your content toward your listeners' knowledge that we will be covering in this section include:

- Build audience involvement.
- Define unfamiliar terms.
- Make statistics meaningful.
- Use analogies.
- Use concrete and specific examples.

Build Audience Involvement

Ask questions, invite comments, or conduct a quick survey to engage your audience in your speech. Keep your audience engaged by using fun facts or provocative questioning when appropriate.

Define Unfamiliar Terms

If you are using technical terms or jargon, make sure you define them for your audience. Do not rely too heavily on these terms if your audience is not familiar with them.

Make Statistics Meaningful

Use statistics that are relevant to your audience and put them in context to make them more understandable. Talk about the impact that the numbers have on people rather than presenting them in a clinical way.

Use Analogies

Analogies can help your audience understand complex ideas by comparing them to something more familiar. Use this to simplify complex concepts when necessary.

Use Concrete and Specific Examples

Use real-life examples and stories to illustrate your points and make your message more tangible. Focus on relatable content that your audience can easily identify with.

Guide your Listeners

To keep your audience engaged and help them follow your message, you need to guide them through your speech.

The tips to guide your listeners that we will be covering in this section include:

- Use previews and summaries.
- Use signposts and transitions.
- Use language that is clear to the ear.

Use Previews and Summaries

Give your audience an overview of what you will be discussing and recap what you have covered.

Use Signposts and Transitions

Use phrases like "next," "in addition," or "finally" to guide your audience through your speech and help them understand how different parts are related.

Use Language That is Clear to the Ear

Use simple, clear language that is easy to understand and avoids complex sentence structures.

Design an Effective Conclusion

Just as the beginning of your speech is important, so is the end.

The tips for designing an effective conclusion that we will be covering in this section include:

- Summarize and refocus.
- Create a closure.

Summarize and Refocus

Recap your main points. A conclusion should summarize your key points and reiterate your thesis statement, providing a clear and concise summary of your argument. Refocus your audience's attention on the main takeaways from your speech and why they matter.

Create a Closure

An effective conclusion should leave your audience with a sense of closure and a clear understanding of what to do next. You can provide a call to action, make a final appeal, or offer a memorable quote or anecdote that reinforces your message.

Conclusion

Public speaking can be a daunting task for many individuals, but it does not have to be. Throughout the five books presented within this volume, you have gained valuable insights and techniques to help you boost your confidence, banish anxiety, and engage, persuade, and captivate your audience by being an effective speaker.

By incorporating these techniques and strategies into your public speaking routine, you will become a more confident and effective speaker, capable of engaging, persuading, and captivating your audience. Remember that becoming an effective speaker takes time and practice, so do not be discouraged if you do not see immediate results. With perseverance and dedication, you will be able to deliver powerful and impactful speeches that leave a lasting impression on your audience.

Glossary

Audience Engagement - The act of capturing and maintaining the interest and attention of the audience during a speech or presentation.

Bad Communication - Messages or signals characterized by lack of clarity, ineffective delivery, or lack of context.

Body Language - Nonverbal communication expressed through physical movements, gestures, and facial expressions.

Charisma - A compelling charm or magnetism that grabs and holds the attention of others.

Confidence - A belief in oneself and one's abilities, often manifested as a feeling of self-assurance and assertiveness.

Confident Individual - A person who believes in their abilities and has a positive outlook.

Insecure Individual - A person who lacks confidence and doubts their abilities.

Influence - The power to affect or sway someone's beliefs or actions.

Persuasion - The act of convincing or influencing others.

Public Speaking - The act of delivering a speech or presentation to an audience.

Public Speaking Anxiety - The fear or nervousness that comes with speaking in front of an audience.

Public Speaking Engagement - A public speaking event.

Self-Confidence - The belief we hold in ourselves and our abilities.

Self-Esteem - Our sense of self-worth and value.

Social Anxiety - An intense fear of social situations and interactions with others.

REFERENCES

Babauta, L. (2007). *25 Killer Actions to Boost Your Self-Confidence*: zen habits. Zenhabits.net. https://zenhabits.net/25-killer-actions-to-boost-your-self-confidence/

Babiak, P., Neumann, C. S., & Hare, R. D. (2010). Corporate psychopathy: Talking the walk. *Behavioral Sciences & the Law, 28*(2), n/a-n/a. https://doi.org/10.1002/bsl.925

Backer, G. de. (2022). Cialdini Principles: *7 Principles of Influence (+ Examples)*. Gust de Backer. https://gustdebacker.com/cialdini-principles/

Barnard, D. (2017). *What are the Benefits of Public Speaking?* Virtualspeech.com; VirtualSpeech. https://virtualspeech.com/blog/what-are-the-benefits-of-public-speaking

Beck, A., Crain, A. L., Solberg, L. I., Unutzer, J., Glasgow, R. E., Maciosek, M. V., & Whitebird, R. (2011). Severity of Depression and Magnitude of Productivity Loss. *The Annals of Family Medicine, 9*(4), 305–311. https://doi.org/10.1370/afm.1260

Bridges, F. (2017). *10 Ways To Build Confidence*. Forbes. https://www.forbes.com/sites/francesbridges/2017/07/21/10-ways-to-build-confidence/?sh=6f0d1ef43c59

Can You Learn How to Be Charismatic. (2020, December 22). Healthline. https://www.healthline.com/health/how-to-be-charismatic

Chen, J. (2022). *4 Types Of Public Speaking*. Www.linkedin.com. https://www.linkedin.com/pulse/4-types-public-speaking-jessica-chen-keynote-speaker

CLIMB Professional Development and Training. (2019, July 9). *The 7 Benefits of Effective Communication in Personal and Professional Settings*. Climb.pcc.edu; Portland Community College. https://climb.pcc.edu/blog/the-7-benefits-of-effective-communication-in-personal-and-professional-settings

Cuncic, A. (2019). *Things to Start Doing If You Have Social Anxiety Disorder*. Verywell Mind. https://www.verywellmind.com/social-anxiety-disorder-tips-3024209

Cuncic, A. (2021). *How to Find Motivation to Overcome Social Anxiety*. Verywell Mind. https://www.verywellmind.com/how-do-i-get-motivated-to-overcome-social-anxiety-3024826

Gaid, A. (2021). *20 Ways to Improve Your Communication Skills*. Www.oberlo.in. https://www.oberlo.in/blog/communication-skills

Gayan, G. (2020, November 17). *What is Charismatic Leadership and Its Benefits?* Nurture an Engaged and Satisfied Workforce | Vantage Circle HR Blog. https://blog.vantagecircle.com/charismatic-leadership/

Gupta, A. (2020). *Self-Confidence| 9 Reasons of Why You lacking it?* Indies Education- Online Learning Library. https://indieseducation.com/lack-of-self-confidence/?amp

Hamilton College. (2019). *How to Engage Your Audience and Keep Them with You*. Hamilton College. https://www.hamilton.edu/academics/centers/oralcommunication/guides/how-to-engage-your-audience-and-keep-them-with-you

Hansen, B. (2022). *4 Reasons Why Communication Fails (and What to Do About It)*. Www.wrike.com. https://www.wrike.com/blog/4-reasons-communication-fails/

Indeed Editorial Team. (2021). *10 benefits of effective communication in the workplace*. Indeed Career Guide. https://www.indeed.com/career-advice/career-development/communication-benefits

Indeed Editorial Team. (2023). *16 Benefits of Perfecting Your Public Speaking Skills*. Indeed.com. https://www.indeed.com/career-advice/career-development/public-speaking-pros

Lebowitz, S. (2015). *7 Ways to Increase Your Charisma, According to Psychologists*. Inc.com; Inc. https://www.inc.com/business-insider/how-to-become-more-charasmatic-according-to-psychological-research.html

Ma, L. (2018). *5 Reasons People Have Low Self-Confidence.* Psychology Today. https://www.psychologytoday.com/us/blog/shyness-is-nice/201812/5-reasons-people-have-low-self-confidence

Manpower Group. (n.d.). *10 Ways to Improve Your Communication Skills*. Workforce-Resources.manpowergroup.com. https://workforce-resources.manpowergroup.com/blog/10-ways-to-improve-your-communication-skills

Martin, E. I., Ressler, K. J., Binder, E., & Nemeroff, C. B. (2009). The Neurobiology of Anxiety Disorders: Brain Imaging, Genetics, and Psychoneuroendocrinology. *Psychiatric Clinics of North America, 32*(3), 549–575. https://doi.org/10.1016/j.psc.2009.05.004

Mayo Clinic. (2021). *Social anxiety disorder (social phobia) - symptoms and causes*. Mayo Clinic. https://www.mayoclinic.org/

diseases-conditions/social-anxiety-disorder/symptoms-causes/syc-20353561

Mayo Clinic Staff. (2017). *7 steps to boost your self-esteem*. Mayo Clinic. https://www.mayoclinic.org/healthy-lifestyle/adult-health/in-depth/self-esteem/art-20045374

Morin, A. (2022). *5 ways to start boosting your self-confidence today*. Verywell Mind. https://www.verywellmind.com/how-to-boost-your-self-confidence-4163098

Murray, R. (2017). *7 Causes of Bad Communication*. Robert Murray. https://robert-murray.com/7-causes-bad-communication/

Musselwhite, C., & Plouffe, T. (2012). *What is Your Influencing Style?* Harvard Business Review. https://hbr.org/2012/01/whats-your-influencing-style#:~:text=From%20our%20research%2C%20we

National Institute of Mental Health. (2017). *Any Anxiety Disorder*. Www.nimh.nih.gov; National Institute of Mental Health. https://www.nimh.nih.gov/health/statistics/any-anxiety-disorder

Raypole, C. (2021). *How to Get Over Social Anxiety: 9 Expert-Backed Tips*. Healthline. https://www.healthline.com/health/anxiety/how-to-get-over-social-anxiety

Simon, G. E., Revicki, D., Heiligenstein, J., Grothaus, L., VonKorff, M., Katon, W. J., & Hylan, T. R. (2000). Recovery from depression, work productivity, and health care costs among primary care patients. *General Hospital Psychiatry, 22*(3), 153–162. https://doi.org/10.1016/s0163-8343(00)00072-4

TC North. (2017). *The 12 benefits of increasing your self-confidence*. Tcnorth.com. https://www.tcnorth.com/building-confidence/12-benefits-increasing-self-confidence/

WPTech. (2020). *Charisma - Why it is important and Why we all have more than we think*. Pinnacle Wellbeing Services. https://pinnaclewellbeingservices.com/charisma-why-its-important-and-why-we-all-have-more-than-we-think/

Exclusive Bonuses

Dear Reader,

I'm thrilled to offer you 5 fantastic bonuses to complement your journey toward mastering public speaking. These bonuses are designed to provide additional support and guidance as you enhance your communication skills and confidence on stage.

Bonus 1: Speak Now: Daily Practices to Master Public Speaking

Discover a collection of daily exercises and practices aimed at sharpening your public speaking skills. From vocal warm-ups to impromptu speech exercises, this bonus will help you build confidence and fluency in your presentations.

Bonus 2: Speak Your Path: Crafting Your Personal Development Plan for Public Speaking Success

Craft a personalized plan for your public speaking journey with this comprehensive guide. Learn how to set achievable goals, identify areas for improvement, and map out your path to success in public speaking.

Bonus 3: Speak with Confidence: A Workbook of Exercises for Public Speaking Mastery

This workbook is filled with practical exercises and activities to help you develop confidence and polish your public speaking skills. From overcoming stage fright to refining your delivery, each exercise is designed to enhance your speaking prowess.

Bonus 4: Checklist for Confident Public Speaking: Essential Steps for Success

Ensure you're fully prepared for your next speaking engagement with this handy checklist. Covering everything from content preparation to delivery techniques, this bonus will help you stay organized and confident before, during, and after your presentations.

Bonus 5: Mindful Speaking: Harnessing Meditation for Confident Public Speaking

Explore the powerful connection between mindfulness and public speaking in this bonus guide. Learn how meditation and mindfulness practices can help calm your nerves, improve your focus, and enhance your overall presence on stage.

How to Access Your Bonuses:

Scan the QR Code Below: Simply use your phone's camera or a QR code reader to scan the code, and you'll be directed straight to the bonus content.

Thank you for embarking on this journey with me, and I'm confident these bonuses will enrich your experience and empower you to become a more effective and confident speaker.

Warm regards,

Kirstin Rae Evans

For feedback, questions, or if you encounter any issues, please visit this link to share your thoughts and get assistance:

https://authorhelpdesk.com/support

Made in the USA
Las Vegas, NV
11 August 2024